Adam Quellin

MICROCARS AT LARGE!

SpeedPro Series
4-Cylinder Engine – How to Blueprint & Build a Short Block for High Performance by Des Hammill
Alfa Romeo DOHC High-Performance Manual by Jim Kartalamakis
Alfa Romeo V6 Engine High-Perfomance Manua by Jim Kartalamakis
BMC 998cc A-Series Engine – How to Power Tune by Des Hammill
The 1275cc A-Series High Performance Manual by Des Hammill
Camshafts – How to Choose & Time them for Maximum Power by Des Hammill
Cylinder Heads – How to Build, Modify & Power Tune Updated & Revised Edition by Peter Burgess
Distributor-type Ignition Systems – How to Build & Power Tune by Des Hammill
Fast Road Car – How to Plan and Build Revised & Updated Colour New Edition by Daniel Stapleton
Ford SOHC 'Pinto' & Sierra Cosworth DOHC Engines – How to Power Tune Updated & Enlarged Edition by Des Hammill
Ford V8 – How to Power Tune Small Block Engines by Des Hammill
Harley-Davidson Evolution Engines – How to Build & Power Tune by Des Hammill
Holley Carburetors – How to Build & Power Tune Revised & Updated Edition by Des Hammill
Jaguar XK Engines – How to Power Tune Revised & Updated Colour Edition by Des Hammill
MG Midget & Austin-Healey Sprite – How to Power Tune Updated & Revised Edition by Daniel Stapleton
MGB 4-Cylinder Engine – How to Power Tune by Peter Burgess
MGB V8 Power – How to Give Your Third, Colour Edition by Roger Williams
MGB, MGC & MGB V8 – How to Improve by Roger Williams
Mini Engines – How to Power Tune on a Small Budget Colour Edition by Des Hammill
Motorsport – Getting Started in by S S Collins
Nitrous Oxide High-Performance Manual by Trevor Langfield
Rover V8 Engines – How to Power Tune by Des Hammill
Sportscar/Kitcar Suspension & Brakes – How to Build & Modify Enlarged & Updated 2nd Edition by Des Hammill
SU Carburettor High-Performance Manual by Des Hammill
Suzuki 4x4 – How to Modify for Serious Off-Road Action by John Richardson
Tiger Avon Sportscar – How to Build Your Own Updated & Revised 2nd Edition by Jim Dudley
TR2, 3 & TR4 – How to Improve by Roger Williams
TR5, 250 & TR6 – How to Improve by Roger Williams
TR7 – How to Improve by Roger Williams
V8 Engine – How to Build a Short Block for High Performance by Des Hammill
Volkswagen Beetle Suspension, Brakes & Chassis – How to Modify for High Performance by James Hale
Volkswagen Bus Suspension, Brakes & Chassis – How to Modify for High Performance by James Hale
Weber DCOE, & Dellorto DHLA Carburetors – How to Build & Power Tune 3rd Edition by Des Hammill

Those were the days ... Series
Alpine Trials & Rallies 1910-1973 by Martin Pfundner
Austerity Motoring by Malcolm Bobbitt
Brighton National Speed Trials by Tony Gardiner
British Police Cars by Nick Walker
Crystal Palace by S S Collins
Dune Buggy Phenomenon by James Hale
Dune Buggy Phenomenon Volume 2 by James Hale
Motor Racing at Brands Hatch in the Seventies by Chas Parker
Motor Racing at Goodwood in the Sixties by Tony Gardiner
Motor Racing at Oulton Park in the 60s by Peter McFadyen
Three Wheelers by Malcolm Bobbitt

Enthusiast's Restoration Manual Series
Citroën 2CV, How to Restore by Lindsay Porter
Classic Car Body Work, How to Restore by Martin Thaddeus
Classic Car Electrics by Martin Thaddeus
Classic Cars, How to Paint by Martin Thaddeus
Reliant Regal, How to Restore by Elvis Payne
Triumph TR2/3/3A, How to Restore by Roger Williams
Triumph TR4/4A, How to Restore by Roger Williams
Triumph TR5/250 & 6, How to Restore by Roger Williams
Triumph TR7/8, How to Restore by Roger Williams
Volkswagen Beetle, How to Restore by Jim Tyler
Volkswagen T5 Camper Conversion Manual by Lindsay Porter
Yamaha FS1-E, How to Restore by John Watts

Essential Buyer's Guide Series
Alfa GT by Keith Booker
Alfa Romeo Spider by Keith Booker
Citroën 2CV by Mark Paxton
Jaguar E-type 3.8 & 4.2 by Peter Crespin
Jaguar E-type V12 5.3 litre by Peter Crespin
Mercedes Benz 'Pagoda' 230SL, 250SL & 280SL roadsters & coupés by Chris Bass
Mercedes-Benz 280SL-560SL roadsters by Chris Bass
MGB by Roger Williams
Porsche 928 by David Hemmings
Triumph TR6 by Roger Williams
VW Beetle by Ken Cservenka and Richard Copping
VW Bus by Ken Cservenka and Richard Copping

Auto-Graphics Series
Fiat & Abarth by Andrea & David Sparrow
Jaguar MkII by Andrea & David Sparrow
Lambretta LI by Andrea & David Sparrow

Rally Giants Series
Big Healey – 100-Six & 3000 by Graham Robson
Ford Escort MkI by Graham Robson
Lancia Stratos by Graham Robson
Peugeot 205 T16 by Graham Robson
Subaru Impreza by Graham Robson

General
1½-litre GP Racing 1961-1965 by Mark Whitelock
AC Two-litre Saloons & Buckland Sportscars by Leo Archibald
Alfa Romeo Giulia Coupé GT & GTA by John Tipler
Alfa Tipo 33 by Ed McDonough and Peter Collins
Anatomy of the Works Minis by Brian Moylan
Armstrong-Siddeley by Bill Smith
Autodrome by S S Collins & Gavin Ireland
Automotive A-Z, Lane's Dictionary of Automotive Terms by Keith Lane
Automotive Mascots by David Kay & Lynda Springate
Bahamas Speed Weeks, The by Terry O'Neil
Bentley Continental, Corniche and Azure by Martin Bennett
BMC Competitions Department Secrets by Stuart Turner, Marcus Chambers & Peter Browning
BMW 5-Series by Marc Cranswick
BMW Z-Cars by James Taylor
British 250cc Racing Motorcycles by Chris Pereira
British Cars, The Complete Catalogue of, 1895-1975 by Culshaw & Horrobin
BRM – a mechanic's tale by Dick Salmon
BRM V16 by Karl Ludvigsen
Bugatti Type 40 by Barrie Price
Bugatti 46/50 Updated Edition by Barrie Price
Bugatti T44 & T49 by Barrie Price
Bugatti 57 2nd Edition by Barrie Price
Caravans, The Illustrated History 1919-1959 by Andrew Jenkinson
Caravans, The Illustrated History from 1960 by Andrew Jenkinson
Chrysler 300 – America's Most Powerful Car 2nd Edition by Robert Ackerson
Chrysler PT Cruiser by Robert Ackerson
Citroën DS by Malcolm Bobbitt
Classic Car Electrics by Martin Thaddeus
Cobra - The Real Thing! by Trevor Legate
Cortina - Ford's Bestseller by Graham Robson
Coventry Climax Racing Engines by Des Hammill
Daimler SP250 'Dart' by Brian Long
Datsun Fairlady Roadster to 280ZX – The Z-car Story by Brian Long
Dino – The V6 Ferrari by Brian Long
Dodge Muscle Cars by Peter Grist
Ducati 750 Bible, The by Ian Falloon
Dune Buggy, Building a – The Essential Manual by Paul Shakespeare
Dune Buggy Files by James Hale
Dune Buggy Handbook by James Hale
Edward Turner: the man behind the motorcycles by Jeff Clew
Fiat & Abarth 124 Spider & Coupé by John Tipler
Fiat & Abarth 500 & 600 2nd edition by Malcolm Bobbitt
Fiats, Great Small by Phil Ward
Ford F100/F150 Pick-up 1948-1996 by Robert Ackerson
Ford F150 1997-2005 by Robert Ackerson
Ford GT – Then and Now by Adrian Streather
Ford GT40 by Trevor Legate
Ford in Miniature by Randall Olson
Ford Model Y by Sam Roberts
Ford Thunderbird from 1954, The book of the by Brian Long
Funky Mopeds by Richard Skelton
GT – The World's Best GT Cars 1953-73 by Sam Dawson
Hillclimbing & Sprinting by Phil Short
Honda NSX by Brian Long
Jaguar, The Rise of by Barrie Price
Jaguar XJ-S by Brian Long
Jeep CJ by Robert Ackerson
Jeep Wrangler by Robert Ackerson
Karmann-Ghia Coupé & Convertible by Malcolm Bobbitt
Lambretta Bible, The by Pete Davies
Lancia Delta HF Integrale by Werner Blaettel
Land Rover, The Half-Ton Military by Mark Cook
Laverda Twins & Triples 1968-1986 Bible by Ian Faloon
Lea-Francis Story, The by Barrie Price
Lexus Story, The by Brian Long
Lola – The Illustrated History (1957-1977) by John Starkey
Lola – All The Sports Racing & Single-Seater Racing Cars 1978-1997 by John Starkey
Lola T70 – The Racing History & Individual Chassis Record 3rd Edition by John Starkey
Lotus 49 by Michael Oliver
MarketingMobiles, The Wonderful Wacky World of, by James Hale
Mazda MX-5/Miata 1.6 Enthusiast's Workshop Manual by Rod Grainger & Pete Shoemark
Mazda MX-5/Miata 1.8 Enthusiast's Workshop Manual by Rod Grainger & Pete Shoemark
Mazda MX-5 Miata: the book of the world's favourite sportscar by Brian Long
Mazda MX-5 Miata Roadster by Brian Long
MGA by John Price Williams
MGB & MGB GT – Expert Guide (Auto-Doc Series) by Roger Williams
MGB Electrical Systems by Rick Astley
Micro Caravans by Andrew Jenkinson
Microcars at large! by Adam Quellin
Mini Cooper – The Real Thing! by John Tipler
Mitsubishi Lancer Evo, the road car & WRC story by Brian Long
Montlhéry, the story of the Paris autodrome by William 'Bill' Boddy
Moto-Cross – The Golden Era by Paul Stephens
Moto Guzzi Sporting Twins 1971-1993 by Ian Falloon
Motorcycle Road & Racing Chassis Designs by Keith Noakes
Motor Racing – Reflections of a Lost Era by Anthony Carter
Motorhomes, The Illustrated History by Andrew Jenkinson
Motorsport in colour, 1950s by Martyn Wainwright
MR2 – Toyota's mid-engined Sports Car by Brian Long
Nissan 300ZX & 350Z – The Z-Car Story by Brian Long
Pass the Theory and Practical Driving Tests by Clive Gibson & Gavin Hoole
Pontiac Firebird by Marc Cranswick
Porsche Boxster by Brian Long
Porsche 356 by Brian Long
Porsche 911 Carrera – The Last of the Evolution by Tony Corlett
Porsche 911R, RS & RSR, 4th Edition by John Starkey
Porsche 911 – The Definitive History 1963-1971 by Brian Long
Porsche 911 – The Definitive History 1971-1977 by Brian Long
Porsche 911 – The Definitive History 1977-1987 by Brian Long
Porsche 911 – The Definitive History 1987-1997 by Brian Long
Porsche 911 – The Definitive History 1997-2004 by Brian Long
Porsche 911SC 'Super Carrera' – The Essential Companion by Adrian Streather
Porsche 914 & 914-6: The Definitive History Of The Road & Competition Cars by Brian Long
Porsche 924 by Brian Long
Porsche 944 by Brian Long
Porsche 993 'King of Porsche' – The Essential Companion by Adrian Streather
Porsche Racing by Brian Long
Porsche Rally History by Laurence Meredith
Porsche: Three generations of genius by Laurence Meredith
RAC Rally Action by Tony Gardiner
Redman, Jim – 6 times world motorcycle champion by Jim Redman
Rolls-Royce Silver Shadow/Bentley T Series Corniche & Camargue Revised & Enlarged Edition by Malcolm Bobbitt
Rolls-Royce Silver Spirit, Silver Spur & Bentley Mulsanne 2nd Edition by Malcolm Bobbitt
Rolls-Royce Silver Wraith, Dawn & Cloud/Bentley MkVI, R & S Series by Martyn Nutland
RX-7 – Mazda's Rotary Engine Sportscar (updated & revised new edition) by Brian Long
Scooters & Microcars, the A-Z by Mike Dann
Singer Story: Cars, Commercial Vehicles, Bicycles & Motorcycles by Kevin Atkinson
SM – Citroën's Maserati-engined Supercar by by Brian Long
Subaru Impreza: the road and WRC story by Brian Long
Taxi! The Story of the 'London' Taxicab by Malcolm Bobbitt
Toyota Celica & Supra by Brian Long
Triumph Motorcycles & the Meriden Factory by Hughie Hancox
Triumph Speed Twin & Thunderbird Bible by Harry Woolridge
Triumph Tiger Cub Bible by Mike Estall
Triumph Trophy Bible by Harry Woolridge
Triumph TR6 by William Kimberley
Unraced by SS Collins
Velocette Motorcycles - MSS to Thruxton Updated & Revised Edition by Rod Burris
Volkswagen Bus Book, The by Malcolm Bobbitt
Volkswagen Bus or Van to Camper, How to Convert by Lindsay Porter
Volkswagens of the World by Simon Glen
VW Beetle Cabriolet by Malcolm Bobbitt
VW Beetle – The Car of the 20th Century by Richard Copping
VW Bus – 40 years of Splitties, Bays & Wedges by Richard Copping
VW Bus, Camper, Van, Pickup by Malcolm Bobbitt
VW Campers, The A-Z, 1950-1990 by Richard Copping
VW Golf: five generations of fun by Richard Copping & Ken Cservenka
VW – The air-cooled era by Richard Copping
Works Minis, The last by Bryan Purves
Works Rally Mechanic by Brian Moylan

Published February 2007 by Veloce Publishing Limited, 33 Trinity Street, Dorchester DT1 1TT, England. Fax 01305 268864/e-mail info@veloce.co.uk/web www.veloce.co.uk or www.velocebooks.com.
ISBN: 1-84584-092-5. ISBN 13: 978-1-84584-092-1. UPC 636847-04092-5.

Readers with ideas for automotive books, or books on other transport or related hobby subjects, are invited to write to the editorial director of Veloce Publishing at the above address. British Library Cataloguing in Publication Data - A catalogue record for this book is available from the British Library. Typesetting, design and page make-up all by Veloce Publishing Ltd on Apple Mac. Printed in India by Replika Press.

Adam Quellin

MICROCARS AT LARGE!

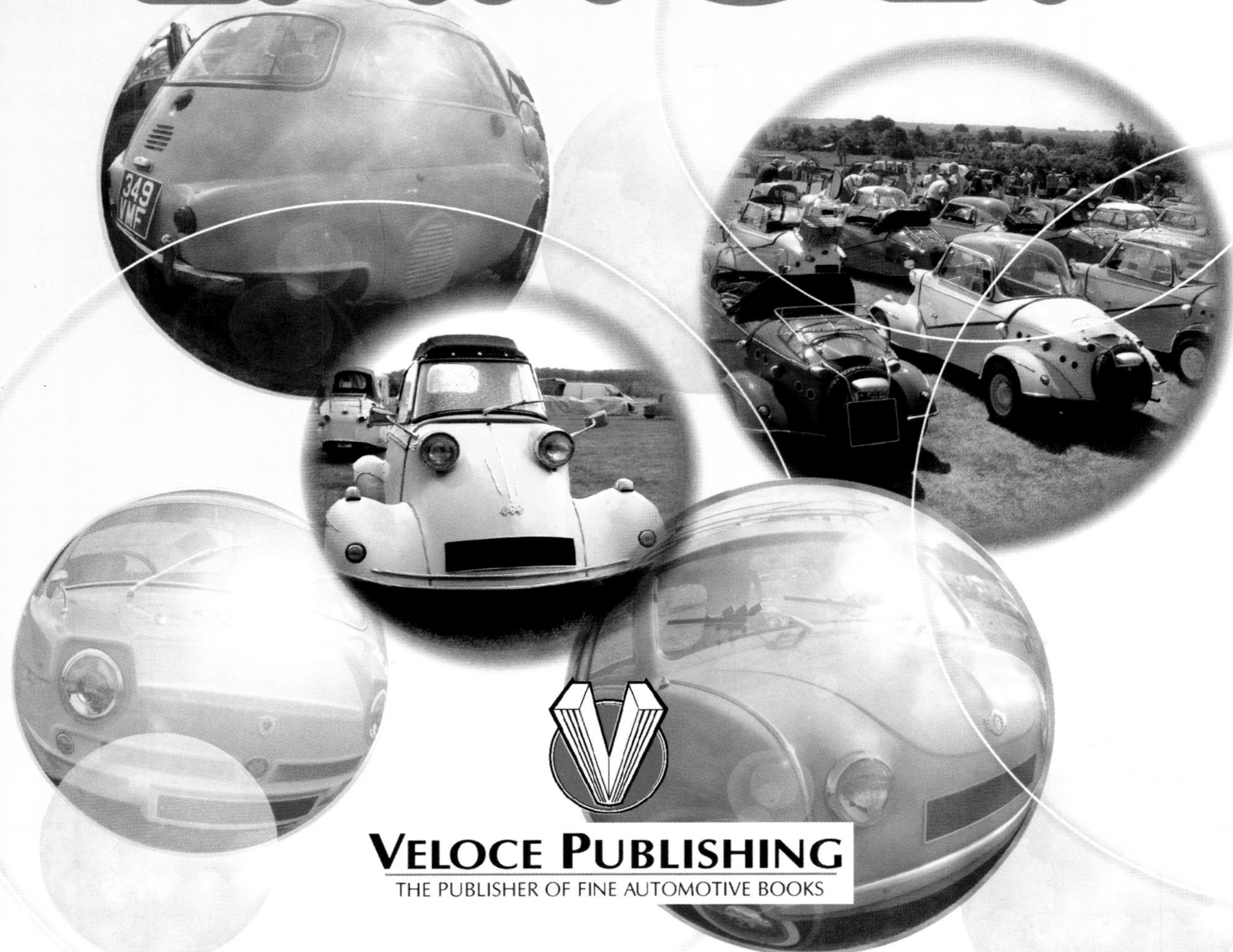

VELOCE PUBLISHING
THE PUBLISHER OF FINE AUTOMOTIVE BOOKS

Contents

Foreword 5
Acknowledgements 6
Introduction 7
Isetta 9
Heinkel Trojan 32
Scootacar.. 50
Peel 56
Bond 61
Reliant. 71
Messerschmitt 75
Goggomobil 89
Nobel.. 93
Berkeley. 97
Microcars today .. .. .103

Index 109

Foreword

It takes patience and dedication to restore and run classic cars. Adam Quellin has that kind of patience and dedication, and has now turned it to a new, but closely-related activity. He has written the story of the microcar.

Aware that the definitive book about microcars was yet to be written, Adam set to work collecting photographs and researching the world of microcars. Six months of writing and a year-and-a-half later, he was ready to gather it all together to create the book you now have in your hands.

The humorous title gives a clue to what lies within – an affectionate and often light-hearted celebration of the smallest and best-loved vehicles on the road.

Of course, Adam's story of the microcar is far from finished. The microcar has an exciting future, and its appeal has shifted from one of economy to the modern goals of space-saving, environment conservation and fashion statement.

But for now, we can be very content with Adam's fascinating history. I hope you enjoy Microcars at large as much as I did.

Martyn Moore, Editor-in-Chief
Practical Classics and *Classic Cars* magazines.

Acknowledgements

I would like to thank the following people for their help and enthusiasm: Malcolm Bull, Andy Carter, John Staine, Dave Hurzon, Ray and Jenny Dilks, Keith Mellors, Neil Foster, Peter Darby, Colin Burton, Lawrence and Jenny House, Peter Jones of the Heinkel Trojan Owners Club, all those owners who allowed me to photograph their cars and Martyn Moore. Finally, a big thank-you to my wife Carol who encouraged me to see the project through to the finish.

Introduction

Small cars have been with us since the early pioneers trundled rickety contraptions out of their sheds. The 1888 Benz was said to be the first practical motor car with its tiller steering and under-floor single-cylinder engine. In the 1920s, it would have been difficult to find a smaller car than the Austin Seven, which took up less space than a motorcycle and sidecar. It is also worth mentioning the Morgan three-wheeler, a precursor to the microcar, with its motorcycle engine up front and bathtub-like construction.

However, this book will focus on cars from the 1950s and 1960s, economy cars which sprang up after the Second World War. These tiny vehicles buzzing around post-war streets were originally known as 'minicars.'

The term 'bubble car' was also used, particularly to describe the rather spherical vehicles, such as the Isetta, Heinkel and Messerschmitt. These minicars and bubble cars were popular with those who wanted to progress from a motorcycle. In the UK, weather-weary bikers took advantage of the licensing laws which enabled them to drive three-wheelers. These small contraptions often used familiar motorcycle components. Some chose to upgrade from the family pre-war car, a minicar being an affordable way to own a new vehicle. The Suez Crisis in 1957 also made small cars with good fuel economy more appealing. Several motor manufacturers, used to making more conventional vehicles, turned their attention to bubble cars. They enjoyed mixed success. BMW did well with its Isetta, whereas Allard did not do so well with the Clipper.

One individual in particular did not find these little cars appealing; Leonard Lord, the cantankerous boss of BMC expressed his dislike by saying "Let's knock those bubble cars off the road." In 1959 the Mini was launched, and no bubble car could

compete with its performance and ability to transport four people and token luggage. It seems ironic now that the new Mini is made by BMW! Bubble cars dwindled until the mid-1960s. Reliant continued to sell well, with its ubiquitous three-wheelers enjoying favourable taxation laws. By this time, they were more sophisticated, with conventional car engines and running gear.

The term 'microcar' was later given to small vehicles which were lightweight, with an engine capacity under 700cc. Microcars often have three wheels, but that is not always the case. The bubble cars and minicars of the 1950s and 1960s were definitely microcars, but there is no hard-and-fast rule. For example, a Bond Bug is always considered to be a microcar, even though the engine size on later models grew to 750cc. There seems to be no strict rule about physical dimensions either. A mini is smaller than a Citroën 2CV or a Fiat 600, but is not considered to be a microcar. So what is definite?

Well, one thing's for sure, microcars never died out completely, and now it seems they are becoming more popular than ever. The tiny Piaggio pickup truck earns a living in places like Italy. The chic and trendy Smart provides nimble transport around many European cities.

The original bubble cars and minicars are now highly sought after and treasured by enthusiasts, with often thousands of pounds changing hands for piles of parts and rust. It seems the microcar is here to stay, with a shift in purpose from post-war necessity to today's owner who enjoys individuality. Here are just a few of the fascinating vehicles which answer to the name 'microcar.' My apologies to enthusiasts whose vehicles I have omitted – there are many and to include these would require a much larger volume. I also hope readers will forgive any inaccuracies; I have often needed to balance conflicting information. Anyway, I hope this book manages to inform, entertain and give you a taste of the world of microcars.

Adam Quellin

Isetta

In 1953, Milan-based scooter and Isotherm refrigerator manufacturer Rennzo Rivolta, turned his attention to the manufacture of bubblecars. Iso developed the Isetta, its name meaning little Iso. Ermenegildo Preti designed the egg-shaped little car, which had an unconventional power unit with two pistons sharing a single combustion chamber. The car's most striking feature though, was the front panel, which opened up as a door. As it did so, the steering column pivoted forward out of the way. The car had a narrow rear track of only 20in across (48cm), meaning a differential was not needed. In 1955, Iso sold the rights of manufacture to BMW, which was in dire financial straits at the time. BMW enjoyed overwhelming success in producing and marketing Isettas and Iso ceased production in 1956. In that year, Iso had only produced a reported seventeen cars and in total, Iso only made around 6000 cars. The Isetta

Isettas pictured at a national microcar rally in England.

continued to be successful with BMW, and Iso went on to produce a conventional light truck. Isettas were never sold in their native Italy; it seems Italians preferred the Fiat 500, Vespa scooters and trucks. Later, in 1962, the company made high-performance cars, such as the Iso Rivolta. The tooling from Iso's Isetta operations was shipped over to Brazil and was used by Americo Emilio Romi to produce the Romi-Isetta Tourisme. Initial Romi-Isettas used Iso engines, however, later cars used the BMW motor. Romi produced 3090 cars made in Spain. Iso also produced the Iso Carro, Auto Carro and Autofurgone models, which were Isettas with pickup and van bodies. These had a conventional rear axle and differential. Velam (Vèhicule lèger `a Moteur) acquired the rights to build the Isetta in France, with major changes to the construction. The bodyshell was redesigned in monocoque form, unlike the BMW version. The engine and gearbox were mounted on a subframe bolted to the body. The engine itself was Iso's own 236cc two-stroke motor. The Velam Isetta had only three wheel studs, like many French cars. The door was opened with a push button on the side, near the headlamp. Inside the car, the speedo was mounted in the centre

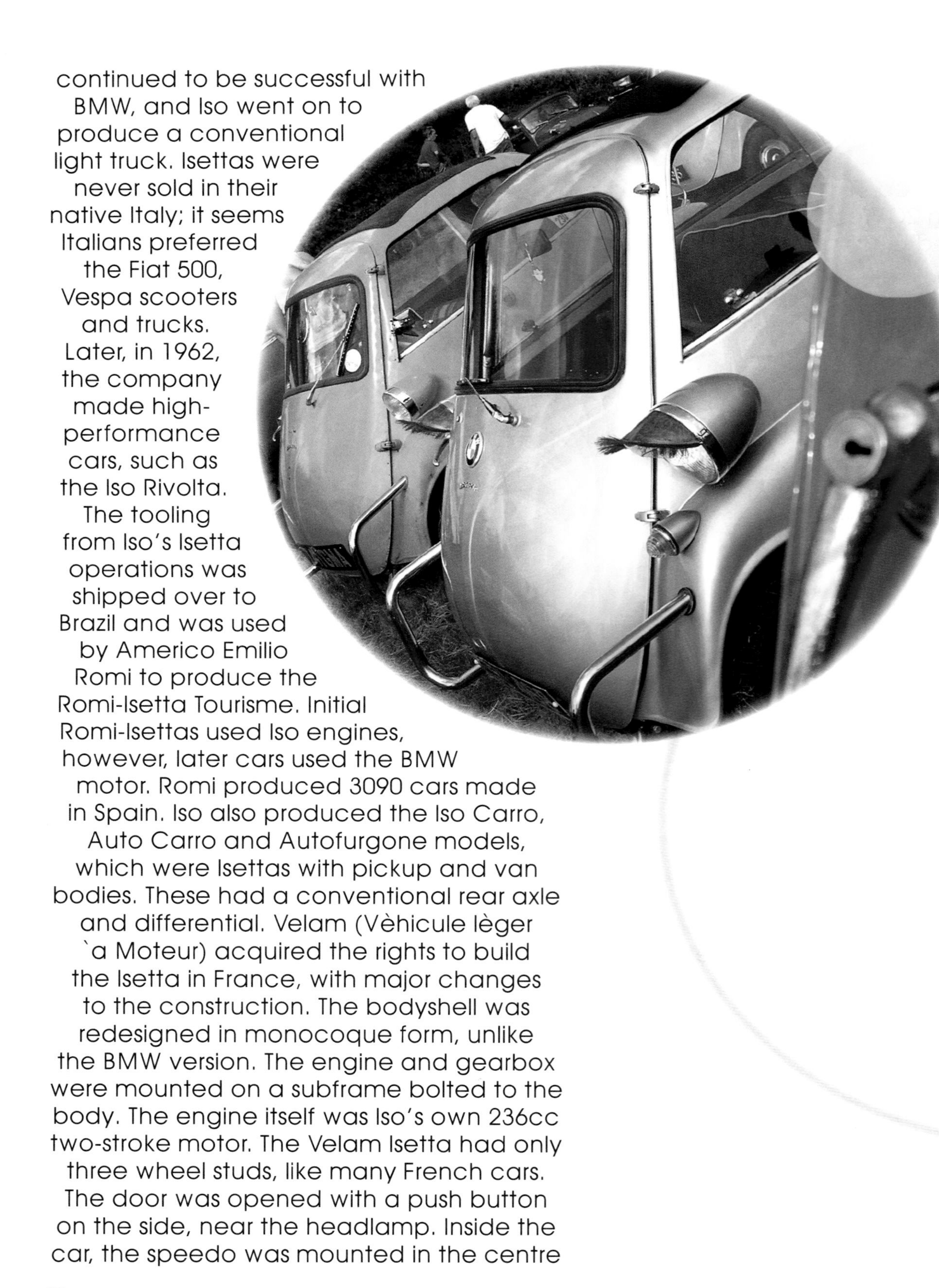

Isetta line-up.

of the steering wheel. There was a more refined version, called the Ecrin, which had a different superstructure.

Unfortunately, the VELAM never enjoyed great success, competing with the likes of the Citroën 2CV and the Renault 750. VELAM ceased Isetta production in 1957, after producing 7115 cars.

The Iso Isetta caught the attention of Jakob Hoffmann, a motorcycle and scooter manufacturer. Unable to obtain a production licence in Germany, Hoffmann adapted the Isetta, changing it in certain ways to avoid legal problems. Thus the Hoffmann Auto-Kabine was produced. The Auto-Kabine was similar to the Isetta, but had a single rear-hinged door on the right-hand side. It used Hoffmann's own 250cc horizontally opposed four-stroke engine, driving the rear wheels via cardan shaft but without a differential. Two prototypes were unveiled to the Press on 2nd June 1954. Delivery of production Hoffmann cars began in September of that year.

Unfortunately, by 1955, legal proceedings forced Hoffmann into liquidation after only 113 cars were made. BMW successfully negotiated the rights to produce its own version of the Isetta in Germany, now that Hoffmann was out of the way.

BMW used its own four-stroke engine, instead of the Iso two-stroke unit. This was a modified version of one of its own motorcycle engines, a 247cc 12bhp single-cylinder type; German licensing conditions favoured vehicles with engines of less than 250cc. This Isetta was called the 'Motocoupe'. Road testers reported a top speed of 54mph and a fuel consumption of 61mpg. For the export market, in 1956, BMW fitted a 295cc engine which had a blistering 13bhp. This was called the BMW Isetta 300. BMW continued to use the narrow track twin rear wheels but also exported a three-wheeler. In 1957, the window arrangement was changed; the bubble type side windows were replaced with one piece sliding glass, which improved ventilation. The BMW Isetta sold extremely well; in 1956 alone, 22,543 cars were sold. In 1957, Captain Ron J Ashley promoted the manufacture of Isettas in England.

Production took place in the old Brighton Locomotive works, which had ended locomotive production in March 1957. There was no road access and all deliveries had to be moved by train. The locomotive staff was retained, and three weeks into the conversion of the factory, the production line was ready. Parts arrived from BMW in Germany and were assembled on a single production line. These British-made Isettas used chassis made by Rubery Owen at Birmingham. The bodyshells were supplied by BMW. The braking system was by Girling and the lighting system was Lucas. German built cars used Hella electrics. All cars were made with door hinges on the driver's side. The first British-built Isetta, like the German versions, were four-wheelers. In around 1958-1959, a Canadian importer went bankrupt and returned a large stock of unsold cars to Britain. These cars were subsequently converted into three-wheelers. This meant a redesign of the final drive assembly, a fairly simple matter in itself. Three-wheeled Isettas had greater appeal to the British motorist, as they were classed as tricycles and attracted a lower tax rate. Another advantage of the tricycle was that if it did not have a reverse gear, it could be driven legally by anyone, unaccompanied, on a provisional motorcycle licence. Unfortunately, the right-hand drive model ended up with the engine and driver both on the right-hand side. Fitting a lead counterweight low down on the left-hand side assured greater stability. This weight was then concealed by the interior trim panel. Isettas were built as three and four-wheelers, the four-wheeler being used for export; BMW of Germany was building Isettas for the USA, whereas only England built cars for Canada. There were saloon, convertible and pickup bodies, at a rate of up to 175 per week.

BMW 600.

Isettas were advertised as being "... the world's cheapest car to buy and run, and ... the easiest car in the world to park."

Isettas had different tyre sizes. German built cars had 4.40x10in tyres. The Brighton Isetta was shod with 4.80x10in tyres, with a 5.20x10 item on the rear of the three-wheeler. There were various trim options too, with tubular type bumpers, resembling towel rails, on the Isetta 'Plus' of 1959. Unfortunately, these tubular vertical bumpers simply bolted through the bodywork at the top, allowing the bumper itself to dent the wing. Later Isettas had larger 7in headlamps. Isettas were put to a variety of uses; a commercial version was used by the RAC until the switch was made to Austin A35 and Mini vans.

A fascinating story involves two Isettas which were used to smuggle refugees across the border from the former East to West Germany. Being such a small car, the Isetta was chosen to avoid suspicion

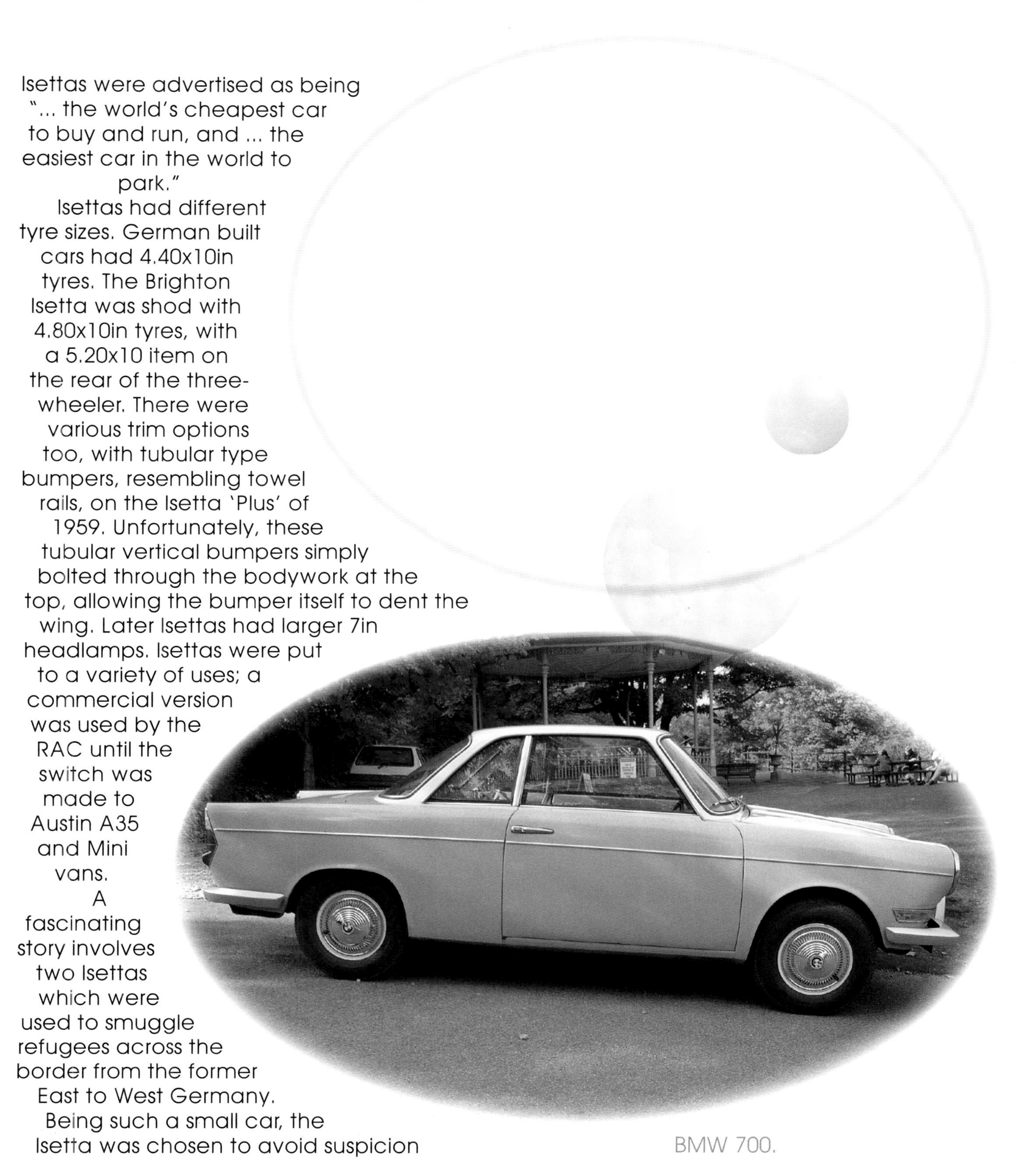

BMW 700.

A bubble window Isetta sunning itself at a microcar rally in Leicestershire. Note the two rear wheels set close together, alleviating the need for a differential.

at the checkpoints. The guards did not realize these two Isettas were converted to conceal a passenger in a special container next to the engine. One Isetta managed six escapes, but the other was caught out on its fourth trip. The car was held up at the border and one of the guards noticed movement from the car. As the driver's papers were being checked, the 57 year-old woman occupant was discovered and both she and the driver were arrested. The other Isetta, the one that eluded capture, is now on display at a

Berlin museum.

In Germany, the BMW 600 was launched in 1957. This was a stretched version of the Isetta and had seating for four people. The rear passengers entered the vehicle by a side door. The original front opening door was retained. The 600 was more refined than the normal Isetta, with a 585cc flat twin-engine developing 19.5bhp.

Inside the cockpit of the Isetta. The interior is basic but functional, with well-made fittings. Isettas are noisy and entertaining to drive. However, Isettas do have conventional controls.

Two sliding window Isettas meet at a microcar rally. The sliding windows offered more controllable ventilation. For a time, both bubble window and sliding window cars were sold simultaneously. The bubble window car was known as 'the Standard' whereas the sliding window car was called 'the Export.'

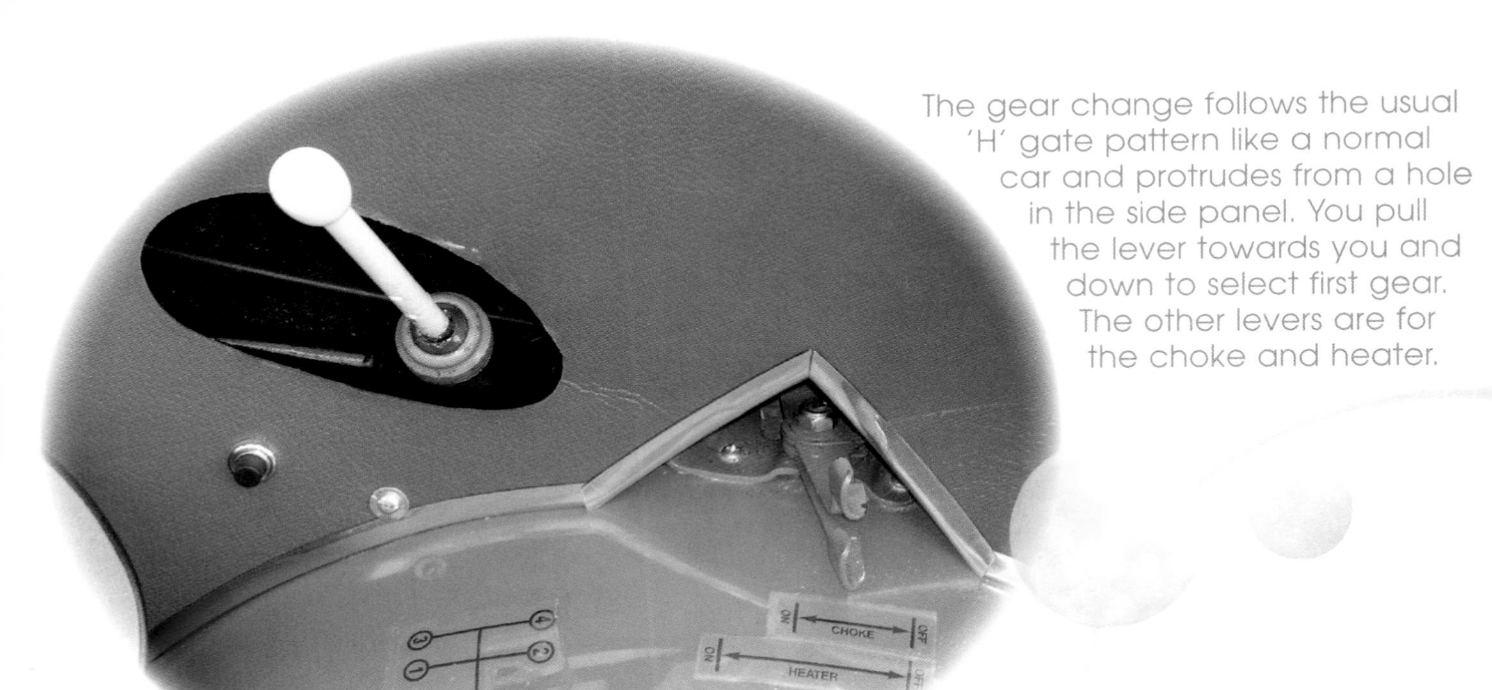

The gear change follows the usual 'H' gate pattern like a normal car and protrudes from a hole in the side panel. You pull the lever towards you and down to select first gear. The other levers are for the choke and heater.

It could achieve 63mph and was therefore better suited to long journeys. It was also BMW's first attempt at semi-trailing arm rear suspension. Production of the 600 ceased in 1959, after only a two-year run, but it sold well. In total, 34,813 were made. Licensed production also occurred in Argentina under the name De Carlo in 1960. The BMW 700 coupè was then

Motive power is from BMW's lively 13bhp single-cylinder air-cooled engine. Underneath that domed cover held on by two screws, are the contact breaker points.

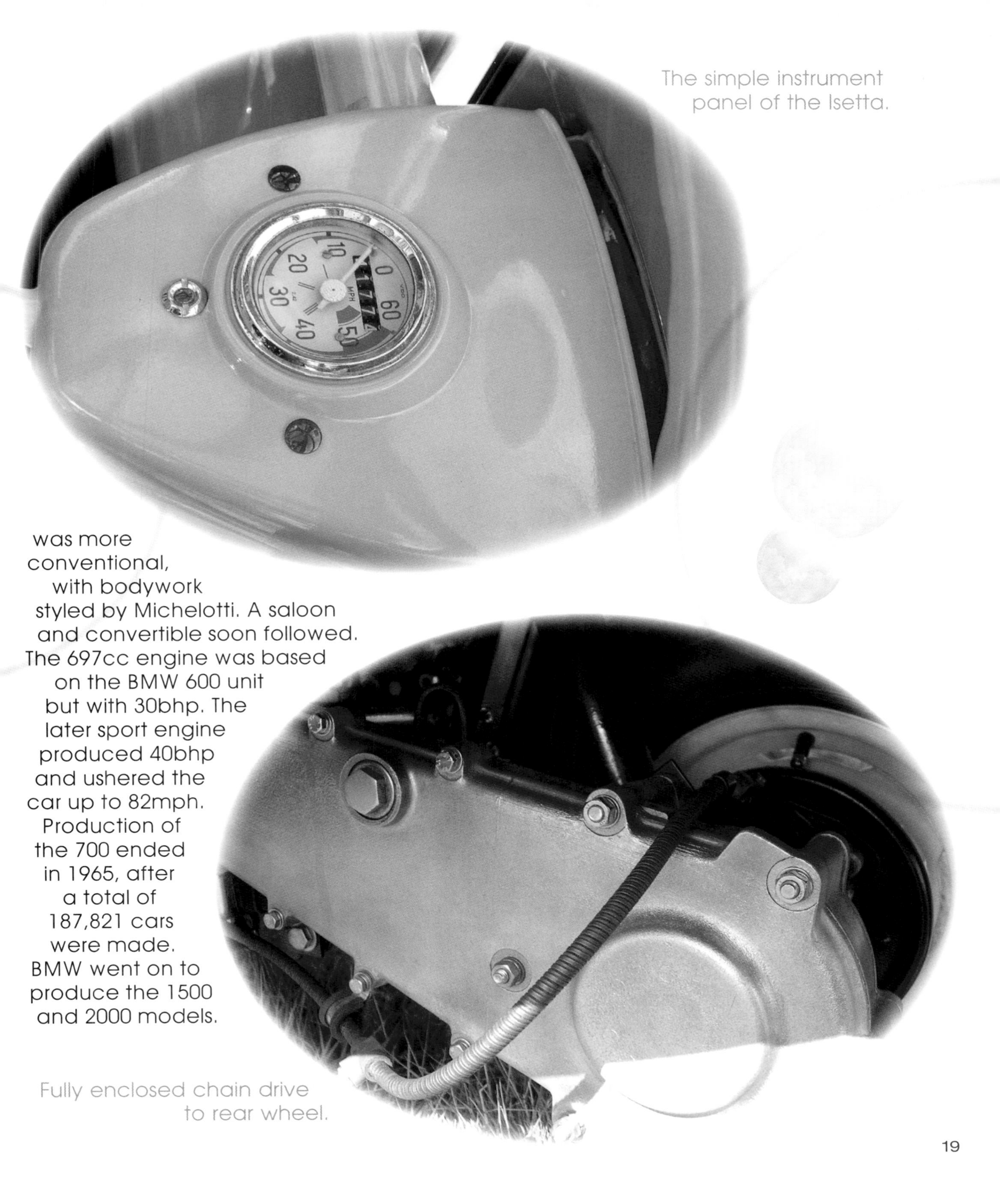

The simple instrument panel of the Isetta.

was more conventional, with bodywork styled by Michelotti. A saloon and convertible soon followed. The 697cc engine was based on the BMW 600 unit but with 30bhp. The later sport engine produced 40bhp and ushered the car up to 82mph. Production of the 700 ended in 1965, after a total of 187,821 cars were made. BMW went on to produce the 1500 and 2000 models.

Fully enclosed chain drive to rear wheel.

A left-hand drive, British-built Isetta.

The company earned the reputation as a maker of quality saloons. The Isetta continued to be made in Germany up until May 1962, with production of the BMW 600 and 700 models running concurrently. By this time, 161,728 BMW Isettas had been built. British-built Isettas (Isetta of Great Britain) continued to produce cars up until 1964. It is estimated a further 20,000 to 30,000 Isettas were made at Brighton. Throughout its life, the Isetta has had many guises. Even the most ardent enthusiast would struggle to recall all the changes made during its history under the hood of his

Semi-circular indicator lens of the British-built car.

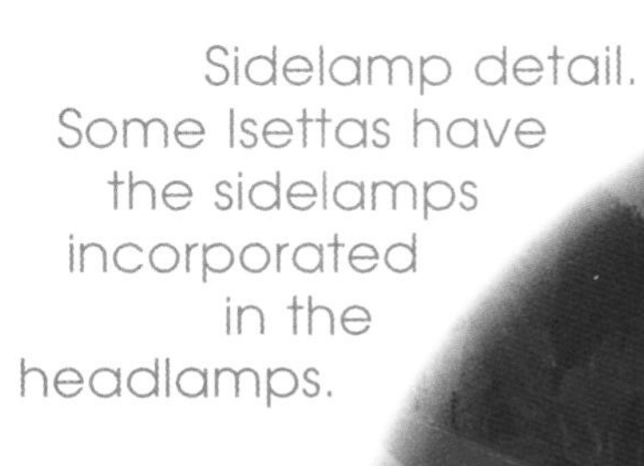

Sidelamp detail. Some Isettas have the sidelamps incorporated in the headlamps.

anorak. There were significant mechanical changes, with BMW ditching the unusual two-stroke Iso engine for its own four-stroke bike engine. There were variations in trim specification, including the bumper designs. Many Isettas were fitted with tubular bumpers, or nerf bars, and looked rather like towel rails. Unfortunately, as they were bolted directly to the front wings, it was the bodywork that got damaged on impact. Famous personalities, such as Cary Grant, were used to gain publicity for

Square Hella indicator lens of the German-built Isetta.

Spot the differences. The car on the right is an Isetta. Next to it is a Trojan 200. Notice the Isetta is much taller and has a smaller windscreen. Both cars are of similar vintage.

Two British-built Isettas. The green example is a four-wheeler for export, and the blue is a three-wheeler. Both cars have the crescent-shaped Lucas indicator lenses mounted on the side, rather than the German-made Hella lamps, which are squarer in design.

The owner of this right-hand drive British Isetta was asking £750 for the car. It would certainly keep its new owner out of the pub for a few weeks! Note the absence of separate sidelamps.

the Isetta in the States. It seems quite surreal, but nevertheless true, that Elvis Presley did own an Isetta, as well as a Messerschmitt. A mail-franking postmark was used briefly in the USA which featured an Isetta. The caption on the postmark read "Greatest economy car in America." Predictably, these small cars were unsuited to the vast

The side indicator lamp unit shows that the car is British-made, even though the lenses are missing. The single-blade bumper tells us this model is an Isetta Plus from 1961 onwards.

highways of America and wore out quickly. Many Isettas were thus abandoned. All Isettas exported to the States were German-made.

Some Isetta facts and figures:
Year of manufacture: 1953-1964
Numbers built:
Iso Isetta – 6000
Velam – 7115
Romi-Isetta – 3090
BMW Isetta – 161,728
Isetta of Great Britain – 20,000 to 30,000

The British Isetta offered a two-pedal driving experience, where the clutch was operated via the gear lever. A magnetic-powder coupling was activated when the gearshift lever was gripped. The 'selectroshift' transmission was not a popular option, even though it was reliable.

German-built four-wheeled Isetta. Note the fixed but curved side windows, compared to the sliding windows of the other Isettas.

The same car viewed from the front. Bubble window Isettas are slightly more bulbous in appearance.

Model types: ISO Isetta convertible, pickup (Iso-Carro, Autocarro 500 and Isetta-Carro), van (Autofurgone), Romi-Isetta Tourisme (with Iso two-stroke engine) and Deluxe (later models with BMW engine), Velam, Ecrin, BMW Isetta four-wheeler and three-wheeler, Germany-bubble side window, later models sliding window. Plus and Standard models, also commercial variants with load platform in place of rear window and luggage area.

Engine type: Iso, Romi-Isetta and Velam – horizontally opposed 236cc air-cooled two-stroke with two pistons sharing combustion chamber. BMW – single-cylinder overhead valve air-cooled four-stroke.

Power output: Iso, Romi and Velam – 10.5bhp. BMW Isetta 250 – 12bhp. Isetta 300 – 13bhp.

Transmission: four-speed synchromesh with reverse. Chain drive (fully enclosed) to rear wheel. Single half shaft from gearbox to chain sprocket with two rubber doughnut couplings.

Detail of front door trim. The trim changed over the years. This badge on a silver door comes from a 1950s car.

This more ornate scripting adorns a later 1960s Isetta.

Detail of the rear panel. The large vent slot shows this to be a four-wheeler.

The louvres found in a three-wheeler, just above the rear number plate lamp.

This immobile Isetta had a crack in its chassis, so it is seen here about to be united with another one at a rally.

Front suspension: Dubonnet.

Rear suspension: swinging arm with quarter elliptic leaf spring and telescopic dampers.

Tyre sizes: 4x4.40x10in (Germany) 4.80x10in (UK) with 5.20x10in on rear (UK models).

Electrical system: CIBA dynastart 12v with contact breaker points.

Sadly, nothing remains of the Isetta factory in Brighton. At the height of BMW

BMW four-stroke Isetta engines were made in Germany by the parent company.

Isetta production, 300 Isetta bubble cars were made per week. The last Isetta was made in 1964. The factory was demolished many years later, making way for a large car park. The car park closed in the 1990s, to make way for a new development, the New England Square. A plaque was recently presented to the site by the Isetta Owners Club of Great Britain.

Note the twin rear wheels set close together on this Isetta chassis.

Heinkel Trojan

After the Second World War, manufacture of aircraft was not allowed. Ernst Heinkel had to wait until 1950 to regain control of his company. However, a prototype motor scooter did appear in 1949. Heinkel commenced building small petrol engines for the Tempo truck. The Tempo was a three-wheeler with the single front wheel driven by an enclosed chain. The engine was mounted above the front wheel. Tempo commercial vehicles were made by Vidal and Sohn, which later had a contract with Heinkel to make bodyshells for the bubble car. At this time, Heinkel also made the 398cc engine for the Champion

Ernst Heinkel thought he could do better after seeing an Isetta, so he developed the Heinkel Kabine (Cabin Cruiser). Heinkel had meetings with Kurt Donath, then boss of BMW, reasoning that his little car was not too similar to the Isetta that it infringed patents. When production was under way, early Heinkels had problems with water leaking in through the front side windows. The problem was not properly resolved, so holes were drilled in the spare wheel well to let out the water.

All round visability is excellent in the Heinkel. The Heinkel has a larger windscreen than the Isetta.

microcar. In 1953, production of the 'Touriste' scooter began. The scooter was a success, with 100,000 machines made at Karlsruhe until production ended in 1965. Heinkel was heavily involved with the development of the 765cc Saab two-stroke engine, and profits from this enabled Heinkel to commence production of his own vehicles. In 1955, Heinkel made his own bubble car, which was similar in appearance to the Isetta. The 'Kabinen' (Cabin Cruiser, as it was known), used a 174cc version of the

Touriste scooter engine, but had a reverse gearbox. This little engine produced 9.3bhp. The car was designated the '150'. Although it looked like an Isetta, the similarity was superficial. The Heinkel Kabinen had no chassis. Ernst Heinkel believed the Isetta to be over-engineered and heavy with its separate chassis. Indeed, Heinkel's prototype was around 100kg lighter than the Isetta. Improvements and modifications were made to the prototype, including some body redesigns. The engine

At the wheel of a Heinkel. Heinkels/Trojans are lively, economical, noisy and fun.

Microcar enthusiast Ted Hilton fills up his very frugal Heinkel.

Front suspension detail.

A lovely line-up of Heinkels and Trojans at a Leicestershire (UK) rally. Note the variations in front badges.

to run with a claimed fuel consumption of 72mpg. In Britain the car became much in demand, especially in the wake of the Suez crisis and ensuing fuel rationing.

The Heinkel was a serious rival to BMW's bubble, so negotiations were made over the design similarity. The advantages of the Heinkel design was a concern for BMW. Heinkel agreed to delay full production of his bubble in the derelict Speyer factory, until March 1956.

Early cars had problems with rainwater leaking inside the cabin, so Ernst Heinkel asked his engineers how the problem was overcome with aircraft. They told him that they used to drill holes in the aircraft floor to let the water out. Heinkel bodyshell manufacture was contracted out to Vidal and Sohn until Heinkel's own facilities were ready for full-scale production. In 1956, the 153 and 154 models were introduced. The 153 had three wheels, the 154 had four. The four-wheeler had the two rear wheels set close together, like the Isetta. Engine size and power were increased to 204cc and 10bhp. By this time, the Zuffenhausen factory was looking to aircraft manufacture again, as this was now permissible in the Federal German Republic.

By March 1957, engine capacity was reduced to 197cc, in line with favourable

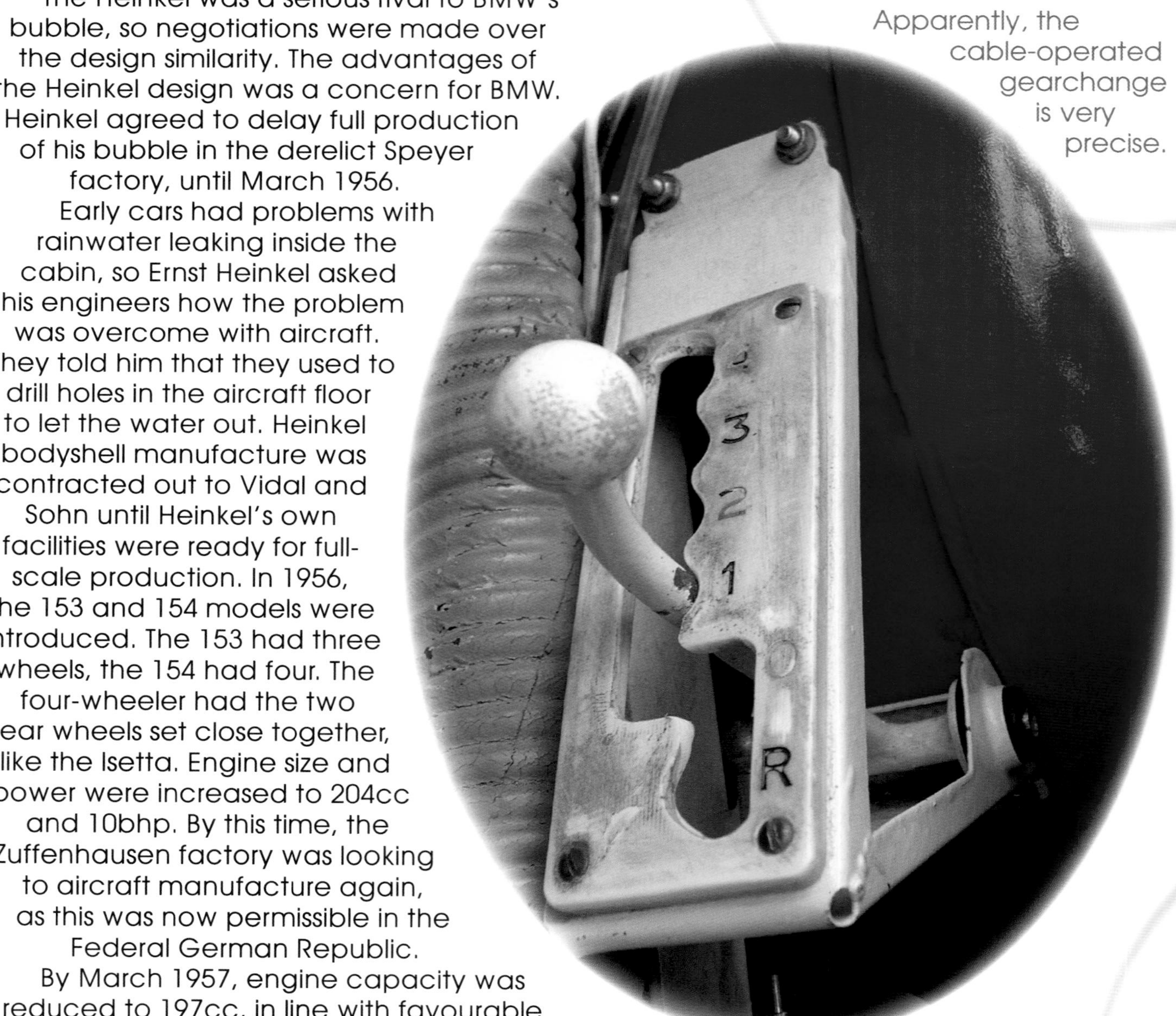

Unlike the Isetta, the Heinkel/Trojan has a sequential gearchange like a motorcycle. Neutral is between first and reverse. Apparently, the cable-operated gearchange is very precise.

The Heinkel controls.

tax concessions. This gave the car a selling advantage over the Isetta, which had a larger engine. By 1958, just under 12,000 Heinkels had been sold. Sadly, this was the year Ernst Heinkel died, aged 70. Assembly of German Heinkels were already taking place in the Republic of Ireland and Argentina. In Argentina, from 1957 to 1961, some 2000 cars were made. These were all four-wheelers, made to compete with the South American Romi-Isetta.

The production licence was sold to Dundalk Engineering in the Republic of Ireland. A convertible was added to the range. At this point, there was still no right-hand drive version and the engines still came from Germany. Around 8000 cars were made at the Dundalk works. There were teething troubles with early cars made in Ireland, largely because the workforce was

Don't forget to turn on the fuel tap.

Heinkels were first made in Speyer, in a derelict factory taken over by Heinkel in 1955. Note the logo on the front door.

unfamiliar with the newly installed equipment, which was not easy to operate. Cars were now sold and marketed by International Sales of Dublin. Heinkel's former UK concessionaire and importer, York Nobel's company Noble Motors, was now without a car to import. So Nobel looked to another German microcar manufacturer, Fuldamobil. York Nobel acquired the rights

When Trojan took over production from Heinkel Ireland in 1961 and built the cars in Croydon, the logo changed completely. It is rumoured that a large badge was used deliberately to hide the fixing holes of the 'Heinkel I' badge.

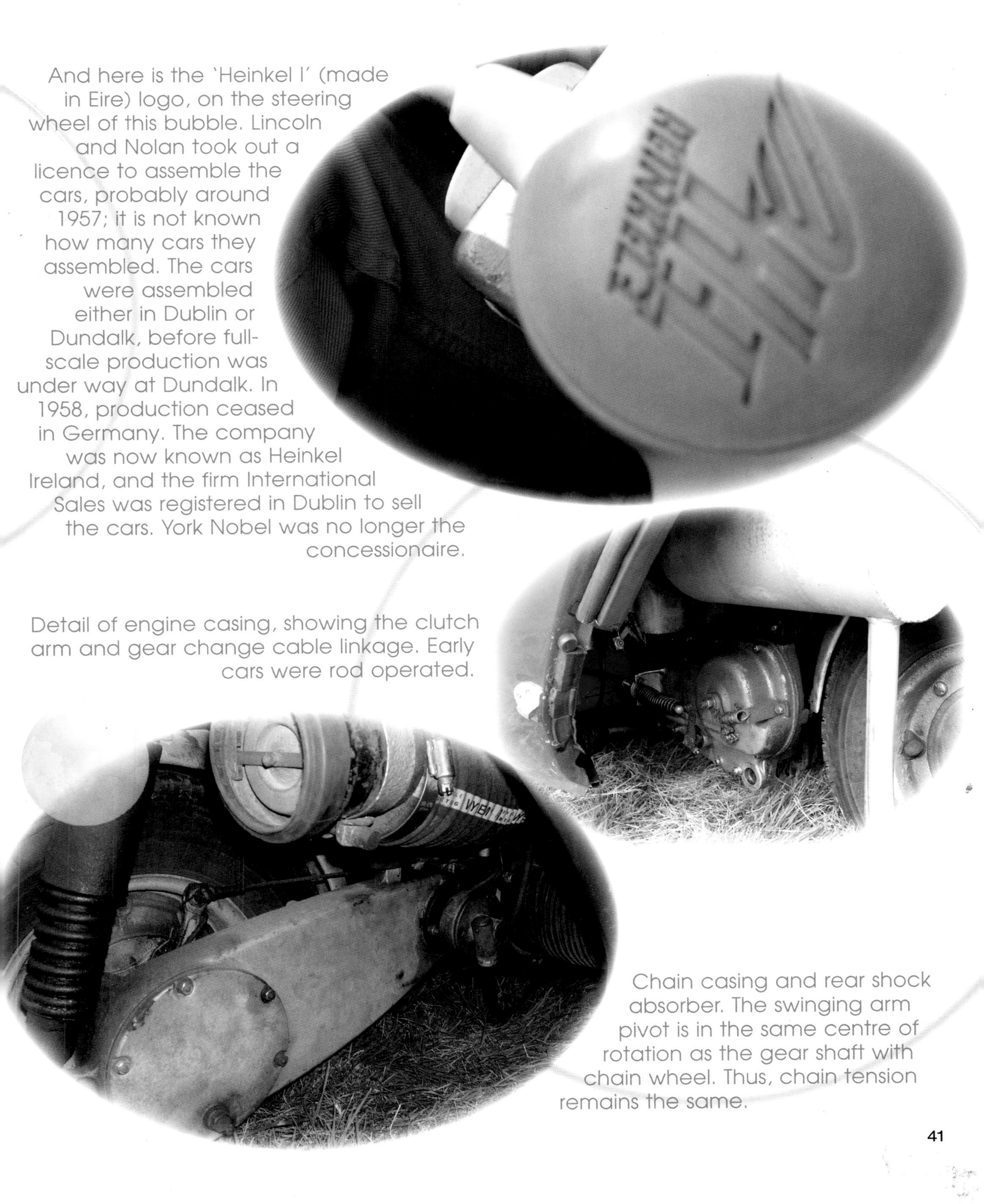

And here is the 'Heinkel I' (made in Eire) logo, on the steering wheel of this bubble. Lincoln and Nolan took out a licence to assemble the cars, probably around 1957; it is not known how many cars they assembled. The cars were assembled either in Dublin or Dundalk, before full-scale production was under way at Dundalk. In 1958, production ceased in Germany. The company was now known as Heinkel Ireland, and the firm International Sales was registered in Dublin to sell the cars. York Nobel was no longer the concessionaire.

Detail of engine casing, showing the clutch arm and gear change cable linkage. Early cars were rod operated.

Chain casing and rear shock absorber. The swinging arm pivot is in the same centre of rotation as the gear shaft with chain wheel. Thus, chain tension remains the same.

"Isetta in front, Messerschmitt at the back" was how the motoring press of the day described the Heinkel. Here, in the present, three Heinkels line up next to three Isettas in the background at a rally. Although appearing similar to the uninitiated, the Heinkel is longer and lower than the more stubby Isetta.

LNT 71C
GB
OFO 329

to produce the S7, which became the Nobel 200.

By 1962, microcar production was in decline, with cars such as the Mini, Fiat 500 and Citroën 2CV proving very successful. The Dundalk Engineering Company ceased Heinkel production. In the same year, the manufacturing and marketing of these little cars was taken over by Trojan, of Purley Way, Croydon. Entrepreneurs James and Peter Agg had just bought the Trojan factory in 1960, for assembly of Lambretta scooters. Trojan had been around as a car maker since 1922, with the Utility, but it had stopped making cars before World War Two. However, it still made the type 15 van, which had a useful payload. These early Trojans had

Heinkel engines started out at 150cc when they first appeared in the scooter. Engine size increased to 175cc and early bubble cars had this engine. A four-wheeled car had a bored out 204cc unit but proved unreliable. Engine size was reduced to 198cc. It is believed that there are three types of 175cc engine – some engines had a three-bearing and others had a two-bearing crankshaft. Early three-bearing engines had the dynastart held onto the crankshaft by a bolt. These bolts caused the crankshaft to crack, so the bolt was substituted with a nut and washer. The engine also had nominal variations in piston size to allow for discrepancies in the barrel dimension. 175cc engines pumped out 9.2bhp at 5500rpm, and 198cc engines, 10bhp at 5500rpm. Car engines of different capacities can be swapped. Unfortunately, the scooter engine cannot be used in the car, because, although the internals are similar, the castings are different. Engines for all Heinkel and Trojan models were built at the Heinkel factory in Stuttgart.

unusual, horizontally opposed, four-cylinder two-stroke engines.

In 1958, the AGG's firm Lambretta Consessionaires merged with Trojan. As a merged company, the Tro-bike, Tro-Tent, Tro-Tractor and Tro-Kart were introduced. Then the formerly named Heinkel was launched as the Trojan 200. By July 1962, over 1000 Trojan 200s had been built, almost fifty a week. Finally, a right-hand drive version was available.

Some Trojans were made for export with twin rear wheels. There was even a van version, although this was in very small numbers – possibly only six or seven. The top part was made of fibreglass and had a door at the back for loading. This was

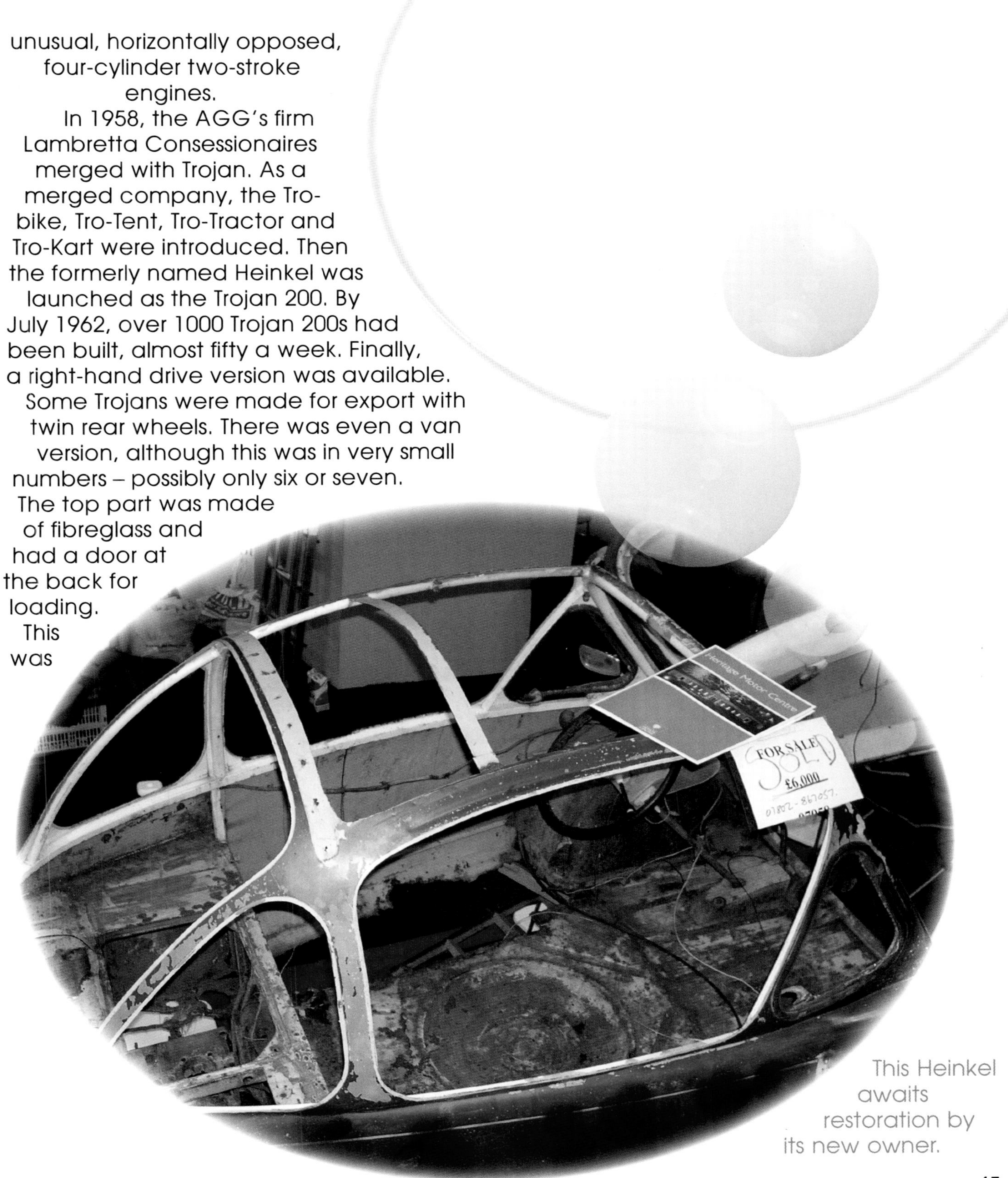

This Heinkel awaits restoration by its new owner.

This smart Trojan interior enjoys the benefit of wall-to-wall carpeting! Unlike the Isetta, the Heinkel and Trojan steering columns are fixed.

produced in an effort to appeal to buyers trying to save money on purchase tax. All Trojans had the 197cc engine. All cars had the door hinges on the left, regardless of whether the car was left or right-hand drive. Unfortunately, this meant those who drove on the left had to exit the car onto the road and the traffic, not the pavement.

Trojan ceased manufacture of the 200 in 1964. Sales were very sluggish towards the end, with some cars not finding buyers until 1966.

The Heinkel/Trojan Owners Club estimates around 26,054 Heinkel/Trojans were made in total, but the company was involved in various other ventures at the time. It made its own go-kart for competition use, called the Trokart. There was also the Elva Courier sports car. In the late 1950s, the Elva sportscar was a race winner in the USA and the car became much in demand. As a result, new workshops in Sedlescombe Road North, Hastings, East Sussex were acquired in 1959. Unfortunately, in 1961, an American distributor failed to pay for a batch of cars and Elva Cars Ltd was forced into liquidation. However, limited production continued until 1962. A reformed company was established by Frank Nichols, and smaller premises at Rye, East Sussex, were secured. The Elva Courier production was taken over by Trojan Ltd Elva cars were made at the large factory in Purley Way, Croydon.

Cars were also designed and built for Bruce McLaren. Trojan carried on with the distribution of Lambretta

Detail of Heinkel instrument panel. Fittings are of high quality. Clock is a wind-up item. The first cars were imported to the UK in July 1956, via Noble Motors of Picadilly, London. The price was £398 15S 0d. It is estimated that around 700 cars are left in the world today, in any condition.

Heinkel's Perle moped sits next to a Heinkel Tourist Scooter at a National Microcar rally in Newark, UK. The moped was less successful than the scooter, in terms of sales. It first appeared in October 1953 at the Frankfurt Motor Show and had a cast alloy frame.

Above: Heinkel Tourist Scooter.
Left: The Trobike, made by Trojan.

An early Trojan Utility from the 1920s. The Utility had an unusual engine – it was a four-cylinder unit but with two combustion chambers and two con rods. Capacity was 1527cc producing 11bhp.

scooters, but by 1965, the firm was only involved in importing Suzuki products from Japan. Trojan had even tried pursuing its own Formula 1 career. The partnership with McLaren ended with the sudden death of Bruce McLaren. For one season in 1973, Trojan had its own racing team. The McLaren M1 was put into production by Peter Agg's Lambretta Trojan Group in Rye, Sussex. In 1970, the Croydon works were sold to the works manager Percy McNally. Trojan Ltd. still exists as an independent company. It has relocated to Effingham Park in Surrey, where it runs a museum conference and exhibition centre.

Heinkels and Trojans are considered by many to be the prettiest of the bubbles.

Scootacar

Designer Henry Brown had previously designed the Rodley, an unsuccessful vehicle which had problems with spontaneous combustion. The Rodley had an enclosed rear engine (a 750cc JAP 'V' twin) which was not cooled sufficiently. When running, the engine caused the whole car to vibrate violently, probably due to poor engine mountings. Not put off by the Rodley's problems, Brown jumped ship and joined the Hunslet Engine Company as new products manager in 1956. Within a year, Brown had developed a prototype four-wheeled car, fitted with a British Anzani engine. This also had overheating problems, but when the car went into production, it was sorted. The Scootacar, as it was now called, had a Villiers 197cc two-stroke single-cylinder engine. It also had three wheels instead of four.

A Scootacar Mk1.

It is said that Henry Brown did an outline sketch of himself sitting on top of a Villiers 9E engine and added everything else afterwards. The resulting car looked very

Scootacars were said to be developed by sketching an outline around a man sitting on top of a Villiers 9E engine; hence the tall aspect of the car. Despite appearances, Scootacars handle quite well.

tall and narrow, but was in fact wider than it appeared. The car handled surprisingly well, with a low centre of gravity. It had a steel chassis and floorpan with a fibreglass body made in two halves. The join ran along the front panel, along the roof and down the rear of the car. A single door was fitted on the left side. The vehicle could accommodate two people, or three at a pinch. Seating was a tandem arrangement, with space for two small people behind the driver. The two-stroke engine worked hard under the seat.

Road testers reported the Scootacar to have good handling characteristics, but it was really put to

The interior of the Mk1 Scootacar. There is plenty of room for storing small items on the front parcel shelf.

the test when an adventurous couple took their car to Istanbul in 1959. Nel and Peter Motte subjected their Scootacar to miles of unmade tracks and rugged terrain, carrying with them all manner of equipment. They wrote a book about their trip entitled *Balkan Roads to Istanbul*. Unfortunately, the intrepid couple hit a bicycle head on and had to abandon the car on the

The controls would be familiar to a Messerschmitt driver. Notice the handlebar.

Villiers 9E engine lurks under the tandem seat in this Mk1 Scootacar.

return journey.

The car was extensively road tested at the MIRA track. Spiritedly driven by one tester, the car rolled onto its front like an egg and righted itself again after completing a somersault. Apparently there was little damage, other than the ride height, which was an inch lower. The Scootacar Deluxe replaced the original model, which afterwards became known as the Mk1. The Deluxe was known as the Mk2. The Mk2 had a more elongated bodystyle, squared off at the tail with a slightly restyled front end. It still had tandem seating and handlebar steering, but the interior was more comfortable. The Mk1 had what was little more than a padded box for the driver to sit on, on top of the engine, with a passenger straddling his legs behind. The Mk2 had a separate front seat, which was set slightly to the right, for two smallish people to squeeze in behind. The engine was now under the rear seat. In 1961, *Motor Cycling Magazine* road tested the Scootacar Mk2.

"The 1961 Scootacar sets a new standard in accommodation for the small three-wheeler. With this go excellent braking, good handling and a sufficiently vigorous performance, to make this little vehicle a very practical proposition

A Mk2 Scootacar lying derelict and neglected in its owner's garden.

A Scootacar does its best impression of a British telephone kiosk.

for the family man who seeks comfortable transport at the minimum cost."

Unfortunately, as microcars were now in decline, sales of the Mk2 were not as good as hoped. Henry Brown left Hunslet in 1960. Little was done to exhibit or promote the product, apart from a sales brochure. In 1961, a more powerful Villiers 324cc twin-engine was installed. Only around fifty or so of these were made. Scootacar production ended in 1965, with around 1500 cars made altogether. Today, many Scootacars survive, due to their durability and the dedication of enthusiasts.

Peel

Peel, the Isle of Man-based car manufacturer, was already in the business of making motorcycle fairings and boats with fibreglass. Around 1955, it made its first car out of this material, the Manxcar (sometimes referred to as the Manxman). The Manxcar was quite a practical little vehicle, with a single rear wheel and a small hatchback-type body. It could carry two adults and two children, or two adults with reasonable luggage space. The car was powered by a British Anzani 250cc two-stroke twin-engine. It was flat out at 50mph, but could do 70-90mpg when driven more sedately. Sadly, only one car was sold and it is unlikely to have survived today. Peel gave up on cars for a while to concentrate on the fibreglass

Trying the Peel P50 for size. Able to fit on the average kitchen table, the P50 was the smallest production car in the world.

Peel P50 prototype. (Courtesy Andy Carter)

mouldings manufacture.

In 1962, Peel was trying its hand at cars again, beginning with a prototype for the P50. The two prototypes were tiny single-seater fibreglass boxes with three wheels. There was a single opening door and a single headlamp mounted on the front. There was no engine fitted to one of these vehicles, and it is rumoured that it was just used to attract publicity and press coverage for the firm. One prototype was actually driven and tested, according to Peel. Having only a single front wheel, the upright contraption was not very stable. Peel developed the vehicle into what became the P50. The wheel layout was changed, so now there were two wheels at the front and a single wheel at the rear. The car was now powered by a 49cc two-stroke DKW engine, sited low down on the right. It was probably the smallest production car ever made, being a mere 52in long and 39in wide.

Around fifty P50 cars were made. Cars were fitted with a three-speed gearbox. There was no reverse, but because the car was so light at only 60kg, it could easily be

Not to be confused with UFO landings, a collection of Peel Tridents are seen orbiting a microcar rally.

The 49cc DKW engine, as found in most Peel P50s and Tridents.

pushed into any small space, and there was even a handle fitted at the back to allow for this. These miniscule motors were noisy and not particularly comfortable. Tiny 5in go-kart tyres made the Peel very skittish on uneven road surfaces, so potholes were to be avoided at all costs.

In 1965, Peel introduced the Trident. The Trident looked like a tiny alien space ship with its bug eyes and Perspex dome bubble. The fibreglass bodywork was made in two sections. The bottom half contained the interior, floor pan and rear section, and the top half was a lifting section with sliding vents on the side. The large clear bubble roof had a flat windscreen attached with a rubber seal. The Trident was a two-seater and used the same DKW engine as the P50, although few cars had a 99cc Triumph Tina scooter (later the T10) engine fitted. In the 1980s, an enthusiast built three replicas. At least one of these was fitted with a Vespa engine. One of the Triumph Tina-engined cars was owned by Peel director Cyril Cannell. Some versions of the Trident had just a single seat, with a container for storing luggage instead. The single-seater option meant that Peels could be driven by 16 year-olds with learner plates. All Tridents had a small stowage area behind the seats. Production of the Trident ended in 1966, after around 90 cars were made.

The interior of the Trident closely resembles that of a pedal car.

Bond

Sharp's Commercials started out in 1922 as a servicing and repair centre, run by motor engineer Paul Sharp. His premises at Lea Garage, Preston, were bought by the Bradshaw group of companies, which later became Loxhams Garages Ltd. Sharp's Commercials also supplied reconditioned military vehicles, but by 1948, this side of the business was running down and therefore had enough floor space to start a new venture. Lawrence Bond was a motor racing enthusiast and knew how to build lightweight vehicles. He built a prototype of his first Minicar, which he called the ⅛ litre Bond Shopping Car. This simple vehicle was of monocoque construction, with an aluminium body and bench seating for two. The engine was a single-cylinder two-stroke Villiers engine of a mere 123cc capacity. It was unusual because the engine was mounted above the single front wheel and turned with it, driving it with a short chain.

A Bond MkA.

Assorted Bond Minicars line-up at a rally.

A Minicar MkD Tourer.

In 1948, Bond teamed up with Lieutenant Colonel CR Gray. It was agreed that 25 Bond Minicars would be made at the Ribbleton Lane works in Preston. Early cars were very basic. The windscreen was made of acrylic sheet – a fairly new material in those days. There was no brake on the front wheel, no suspension at the rear. and steering was by cable and bobbin. This setup proved to be unreliable and possibly dangerous. This method was later replaced with a safer rack system. A large pull handle under the dashboard acted as a starter, thus turning the engine manually. An under-bonnet kickstart was also available as a backup measure. Later cars were equipped with electric starters. Despite its crudity, the Minicar was snapped up by motorists eager to acquire a cheap new car which cost little to run. After nearly 2000 minicars were made, the MkB arrived on 1st July 1951. The MkB looked similar to the first minicar, which became known latterly as the MkA. However, the MkB had a larger 197cc engine which gave the vehicle a notable improvement in performance. MkBs also had rear wheel suspension and a windscreen made of safety glass. There was now a Sharp's minitruck and minivan for the commercial fleet. The Bond Minicar Family Safety Saloon was also launched, which was similar to the minivan, but had two hammock-style rear seats facing each other, so children could sit sideways.

The Safety Saloon also had rear side windows. There were no interior rear door handles, presumably to stop inquisitive fingers from opening the door while the vehicle was in motion

Production of the MkB came to an end in December 1952, but 1953 saw the arrival of the MkC. The MkC had a very different front end with dummy wings sprouting up either side of the long bonnet. The large frontal area allowed room for the engine and front wheel to turn 180 degrees lock-to-lock, which enabled the car to perform amazingly tight manoeuvres, as the car could turn in its own length. Bond Minicar enthusiasts at car rallies seem to enjoy spinning their cars round and round on-the-spot like dodgem cars, much to the amusement of onlookers. The headlamps on the MkC were now mounted in the front wings, and brakes were now fitted on all three wheels. Some MkC Minicars had glassfibre hard-tops. In 1956, production of the MkC came to an end after 6500 cars were made. The MkC

The MkD, like many other Bonds, was powered by a 197cc Villiers engine. The amount of space around the engine allows the whole engine/transmission to pivot with the front wheel. These engines have no fan to keep them cool, but simply rely on the passage of cool air through the grille and over the cooling fins. Minicars can overheat if climbing slowly up a hill in a low gear for a prolonged period.

offered practical motoring at minimal cost for many people. One of the slogans Sharp's Commercials used in its brochures was 'Time is money – can you afford to walk?'. These cars often had a hard life. The Sharp's factory had its own MkC minivan which was used to deliver spare parts to dealers. The vehicle racked up 100,000 miles in under ten years, earning its keep. Unfortunately, compared to other Bonds, not many MkCs survive.

Then the MkD arrived and not long after, the MkE. The MkE appeared in December 1957 and was made alongside the MkD. Eight prototype MkEs were made in 1956, although it was December 1957 when full-scale production began. Handling problems had to be ironed out by widening the rear track and flaring the wheel arches. The wheelbase was also lengthened. The MkE had a full width front end design, which made it more modern in appearance. Both cars continued to be made side-by-side until November 1958, when the MkF was introduced. 1180 MkEs were made. Some MkDs were shipped to the USA, to be sold by Craven and Hendrick of New York. The car was designated the Sharp's Bearcub. The project was not a great success, as few cars were sold. It seems hardly surprising, in the vast open spaces of America, that there

Minicar MkG with raked-back rear window and front quarterlights.

would be little demand for these small cars. Some MkDs were shipped to Australia.

The MkF of 1958 was not very different externally from the MkE. However, it now had the Villiers 31A 250cc two-stroke engine. The car could now achieve a useful 55mph.

MkF variants consisted of Family Saloon, Ranger van, convertible two-seat Tourer and Coupé.

The Ranger van was appealing to buyers in that they didn't pay purchase tax. The downside was the speed was restricted to 30mph as it was a commercial vehicle. MkFs were larger than previous Bonds, but still only offered limited accommodation. The hammock seats were still being used for rear passengers.

The Minicar MkG Estate is a useful load carrier.

In 1961, the MkG arrived. This was the last Bond to have the engine mounted over and driving the front wheel. The MkG was a proper four-seater, with a higher roofline and raked-back rear window, similar to the Ford Anglia or Reliant Regal. It had hydraulic Girling brakes and 10in wheels. New independent trailing arm rear suspension with telescopic shock absorbers was the order of the day. Passengers now also benefited from swiveling vent windows. A MkG Estate and Ranger van was available. These had useful rear tailgates.

In March 1963, buyers had the option of the Villiers 4T twin-cylinder two-stroke engine of 250cc, or they could have the standard 250cc single-cylinder.

The Bond 875 was a completely new

machine. In August 1965, the MkG Minicar was still being made but seemed archaic in comparison. In place of the Villiers motorcycle engine, the 875 had a sting in the tail in the form of the Hillman Imp engine. The 875 was fast. Racing driver John Surtees drove a prototype around Brands Hatch and almost reached 100mph. The decision was made to fit a detuned version of this engine to these cars. Even so, the 875 was still able to achieve close to 80mph and 50mpg. A van version was also available without side windows, but with a useful rear-load hatch. In 1968, the car was given a facelift with minor cosmetic changes, including rectangular headlamps. The Bond 875 was much more like a conventional car than previous models, but sales figures were disappointing. The 875 was discontinued in 1970.

The Bond Bug made its striking appearance in the same year. A high profile ceremony took place in June of that year at Woburn Abbey for the orange wedge on wheels. The car used standard Reliant Regal mechanicals but had a sporting image, thanks to the low-slung two-seater bodyshell with lift-up canopy. The result of the Ogle Design Studio, with Tom Karen as Managing

In August 1965, the Bond 875 made its debut. It was very different from all the other three-wheeled Bonds. A Hillman Imp engine was situated at the rear and the car had an all new fibreglass bodyshell. Racing driver John Surtees tested a pre-production 875 and nudged the car up to 100mph. There was also a Ranger van model, for those who wanted to avoid purchase tax, but again, drivers had to put up with a 30mph restriction. March 1968 saw the Mk2 875, which had a restyled front end. The basic shape remained the same, albeit with a few detail changes such as rectangular front headlamps. Seating was improved. Bond was bought by arch rival Reliant in 1969. The Bond 875 was made up until 1970.

The Bond 875 interior is unashamedly Hillman Imp, apart from the steering wheel.

The engine is the Imp all-alloy unit, seen here in the 'car' version of the Bond 875. The Ranger van has a useful rear hatch with the engine under a panel. Sadly, not many 875s survive, compared to other Bonds.

Director, was that the Bug appealed to young trendy people, looking for a chic three-wheeler. Reliant used many celebrities to promote Bug sales, thus adding a touch of glamour. Early cars were built at Preston and were transported to Tamworth for finishing.

The Preston factory was soon closed down and full-scale production carried on at Tamworth. The wedge-shaped bodywork was only available in tangerine, as the colour was officially known. There were a few exceptions to this. A small number of Bugs were painted different colours for promotional use. There were three versions of the Bond Bug. There was the Bug 700, which didn't have the sidescreens, the Bug 700E which had a heater, sidescreens, telescopic damper lifting canopy, driver's sun visor and courtesy light. Then there was the Bug 700ES, which in addition to those refinements, had a higher compression engine, alloy wheels and mud flaps. The ES used the higher compression Regal/Rebel engine which produced 31bhp and could achieve just over 77mph. Other Bugs used the standard 29bhp engine. Only one standard Bug 700 was actually made. From October 1973, Bugs were fitted with the 748cc engine. They were now designated the 750E and 750ES, but out of a total of 2270, only 142 were sold. Bug production ended in May 1974, and the very last Bugs were registered in 1975.

Bond Bug lifts its lid.

Reliant

In 1935, former works manager for Raleigh (who produced the Safety Seven) TL Williams, built a prototype in the garden of his home in Kettlebrook, Tamworth, UK. This vehicle was a three-wheeled van powered by a 600cc JAP engine. In 1937, when Williams had established the Reliant company, his firm was supplied with Austin Seven engines.

In 1939, Reliant made its own engines based on the Austin Seven unit. In 1940, Reliant stopped producing motor vehicles to concentrate on parts machining for the war effort. By 1946, the firm was producing vehicles again. In 1952, the Reliant van was modified into a car for carrying passengers, called the Regal. Sadly, only two Mk1 Regal cars are known to exist today. One is on display at the National Motor Museum at Beaulieu, Hampshire, UK.

The Mk1 Regal had aluminium bodywork with an ash frame. In 1955, the Regal Mk2

A Raleigh Safety Seven – a sort of great uncle of the Reliant Robin.

An early Reliant Regal – possibly a Mk4.

arrived, with fibreglass body panels. Reliant was able to keep the weight down on its vehicles to under 8cwt, the maximum weight limit for a three-wheeled car to be eligible for road tax at the motorcycle rate. In 1956, the Regal Mk3 was introduced. This was the first Reliant to have bodywork completely made of fibreglass. The Mk4 arrived in 1958 and featured 12 volt electrics and flashing indicators. The Mk4 also had balanced lift drop-side windows, superceding the earlier sliding windows. The Mk5 arrived in 1959, with minor changes to the interior, bodywork and wheelbase. Mk5 cars reverted to the earlier system of horizontally sliding windows. After only a year in production, the Mk6 arrived in 1960, with a revised roofline, combined stop/tail lamps and revised dashboard.

In 1962, the revolutionary Regal 3/25 came, with angular styling and an all new overhead valve alloy engine, developed by Reliant. The 3/25 had one-piece fibreglass bodywork mounted on a steel chassis. During this time, the older Mk6 continued in production for a few months, using the new engine. In 1964, the Rebel was introduced, a four-wheeled version of the Regal with different front-end styling. It was not as popular as the Regal, because it was regarded by many as overpriced compared to other small four-wheeled cars, and also didn't enjoy the tax benefits of the three-wheelers. In 1969, the car was given a useful power boost from a new 700cc engine. By this time, 50,000 Regal 3/25s had been sold. The car was now called the Regal 3/30. Reliant also produced fibreglass truck cabs for other companies, such as Scammel. In 1967, Reliant produced a new commercial three-wheeler vehicle, the TW9. The TW9, later known as the Ant, had a single front wheel of semi forward control design, with a steeply sloping frontal area and an engine protruding into the cab. In 1977, production rights of the TW9 – which stood for three wheels – were sold to BTB Engineering Ltd. Meanwhile, Reliant had launched the all new Robin in 1973. Designed by Ogle Design, the people who created the Bond Bug, the Robin was very different from the Regal in appearance.

The Robin had a more curved, rounded look, bringing it more up-to-date. The engine was now a 750cc unit, producing 32bhp. Robins were available as a saloon, estate or van. In 1975, the engine capacity had increased to 850cc and the old Zenith carburettor was replaced by an SU type. Brake horsepower was now rated at 40, offering lively performance. Princess Anne bought a Robin Super Saloon whilst living at the Sandhurst Royal Academy. There was even a

A late model Reliant Robin.

A Regal 3/25.

four-wheeler called the Kitten. In 1981, the Robin was replaced by the Rialto, a more squared-off looking car with square headlamps and plastic grille. As time progressed, Reliant found itself in financial difficulties and by 1990, the receivers were called in. In October of the same year, the company was bought by Bean Engineering for £1.5 million. In 1993, a new range of Robins was introduced, however, success was short lived, as Bean called in the receivers in November 1994. On 16th January 1995, the Reliant name was saved again, this time by the Avonex Group. Unfortunately, the company was in trouble yet again and by December 1995, the receivers were called in once more. In April 1996, Reliant was purchased by an optimistic consortium of businessmen. Business picked up again and in August of 1996 Reliant Robin production resumed. By August the following year, 720 cars had been built. Production ceased at Tamworth in late 1998, and in January 1999 the company moved to new premises at Burntwood. Reliant expanded into lightweight commercial vehicles and was involved in import and distribution of vehicles, such as the Ligier microcar from France. They also imported the Piaggio Ape truck from Italy. February 1999 also saw the arrival of a new Robin hatchback, capable of 60-100mpg. By 2000, on 26th September, Reliant announced it would stop making three-wheelers. To celebrate 65 years of making three-wheelers, 65 special edition Robins were made, not surprisingly, these cars were called the Robin 65. These special Robins were lavishly appointed with an individual numbered plaque on each car's dashboard. Robin 65s also sported a leather interior trim, gold metallic paint and alloy wheels. A top quality stereo system also kept the Robin on song. At £10,000, these Robins were not cheap. Every prospective owner was invited to the Reliant premises to collect their new car, have a tour of the factory and even got to meet the person who made their car. The last Robin 65 was won as a prize offered by the *Sun* newspaper, on 14th February 2001. Reliant car production then moved to Cannock, UK. The company is now trading as Reliant Parts World Ltd, where it deals in spare parts and continues to import Italian Ape trucks and Ligier microcars. Reliant also imports a few motorcycles. There have also been rumours of a new sports car, but this is unconfirmed. Other Reliant cars worthy of note are the Turkish-built Reliant Anadol, similar in concept to the Bond Equipe and the Scimitar, which used the Ford V6 engine. Scimitar production took place from 1964 to 1986. However, 77 cars were built to order afterwards by two businessmen enthusiasts – these cars were known as the Middlebridge Scimitars. In 1991, there was the Nissan-powered SS1, but this was not as successful in terms of sales as the Scimitar. Reliant is now owned by Glen Investments.

Messerschmitt

Designer Fritz Fend worked at the Messerschmitt aircraft factory during World War Two and was involved in the development of Germany's first jet aircraft. After the war, Fend moved to Rosenheim to take over the running of his father's shop, and while he was there, he thought about designing a new form of transport.

Working on a covered pedal-powered tricycle, he experimented with a unique gearing system. He performed experiments himself by traversing a flight of stairs, carrying different weights to work out the gearing he would need. He observed the amount of effort required with different loads and taking one, two or three steps at a time. Fend started building a working model, but his efforts were frustrated by the lack of materials available at the time. Placing his ideas on hold, he concentrated on the family business.

A KR 200 on the left and a KR 175 with faired-in-front wings on the right.

GB

A squadron of
Messerschmitts at a rally.

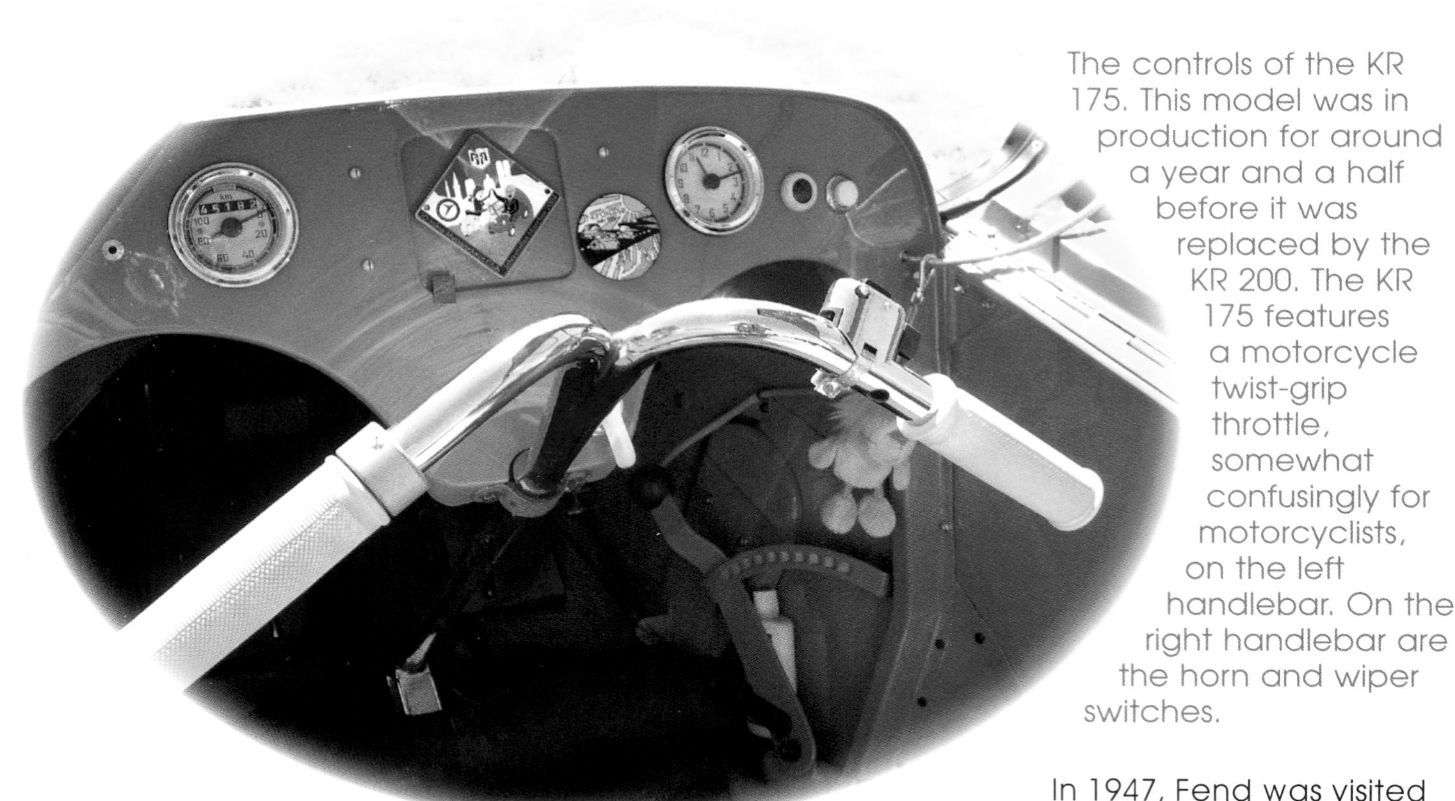

The controls of the KR 175. This model was in production for around a year and a half before it was replaced by the KR 200. The KR 175 features a motorcycle twist-grip throttle, somewhat confusingly for motorcyclists, on the left handlebar. On the right handlebar are the horn and wiper switches.

In 1947, Fend was visited by a war veteran who had lost both legs. Fend made him a small tricycle with a single seat and steering lever. The lever propelled the vehicle by the operator pushing and pulling on it in a sort of rowing action. This trike attracted the attention of the War Wounded Association who were impressed by the machine and ordered fifty vehicles. Unfortunately, the payment wasn't enough to boost Fend's business. He went on to develop a similar tricycle with covered bodywork. The Association liked the new tricycle, as did the Ministry of Labour in Munich. Fend was able to produce the vehicle with proper materials.

Fend was looking towards another form of motive power, and in 1948 he bought a power-assisted bicycle which had a 35cc Victoria engine bolted onto it. He then cannibalized the bike for his next project, a new trike which achieved 40km/h.

Fend developed a good business relationship with the Fichtel and Sachs engine company and used its 100cc engine in another tricycle. At this point, he was finding that the bicycle-type wheels were flimsy with this extra power, so he looked towards other sources. Car wheels would have been too bulky and heavy for the lightweight machine, which was now known as the Flitzer – which literally means something that flits about. A combination of wheelbarrow wheels at the front and the power-assisted bike wheel at the rear was tried. Fortunately, a more satisfactory solution was found when Fend persuaded Dunlop to make small tyres to fit his cars. All three wheels became the same size and Fend developed the braking and suspension.

A business partner was found who could invest in the fledgling company and help it expand. Fend needed this, as he was limited in the amount of vehicles he could produce himself. Unfortunately, the arrangement didn't work well, as the partner got the main share of the profits. Eventually, Fend contacted his old employer, Professor Willi Messerschmitt of Regensburg.

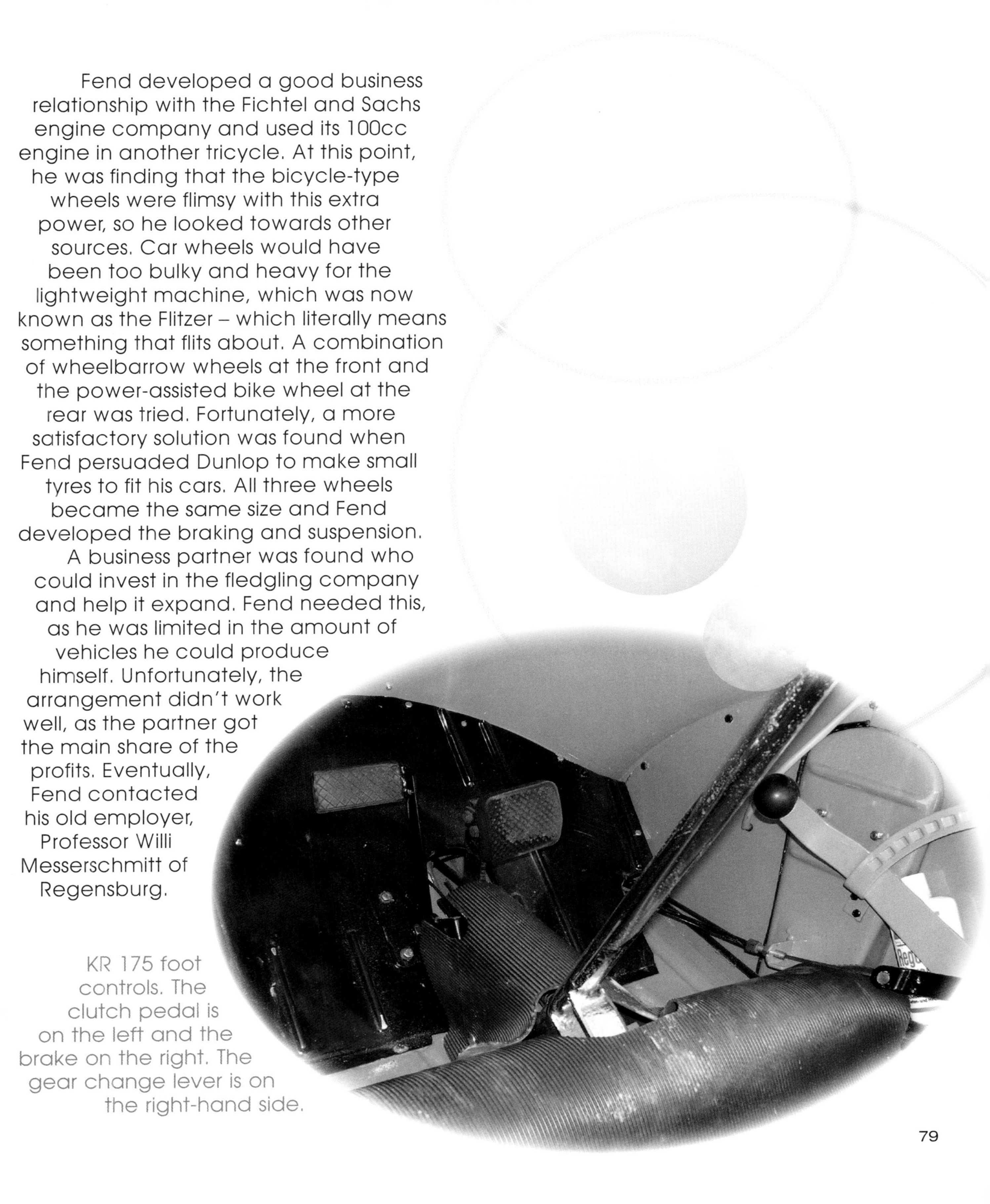

KR 175 foot controls. The clutch pedal is on the left and the brake on the right. The gear change lever is on the right-hand side.

A very stylish trailer from Eastern Europe was sourced for this Messerschmitt and painted in the appropriate colour. Seems like car and trailer were made for each other.

Messerschmitt was not permitted to build aircraft, as dictated by the post-war situation. Instead, his company was involved in engineering projects and the repair of railway rolling stock. Messerschmitt was keen to do business with Fend and together they discussed the idea of a three-wheeled car with tandem seating. This new vehicle would have a plexiglass domed canopy, which swung open to allow access to the inside. In 1952, Fend and Messerschmitt formed a partnership and by the summer of that year, the Fend Kabinenroller (Cabin scooter) FK 150 prototype was made.

By 1953, the car was made available to the public and was displayed at the Geneva Motor Show. Later, the KR 175 appeared. The domed canopy was an innovation in motoring circles, reminiscent of aircraft days. In total, 11,000 KR 175s were made from 1953-1955. The KR 175 received criticisms from motorists, complaining of noise and vibration. Fend looked to remedy this and in February 1955, the KR 200 was launched. The KR 200 was a big improvement over the earlier car. It had a wrap-around windscreen – although this was just introduced on late KR 175 cars. It had new cut out wheel arches to allow the front wheels to turn a greater arc, thus improving the turning circle.

The front track width was also increased. KR 200s now had rubber in torsion suspension with telescopic dampers. KR 175 drivers had to make-do with a large spring under the driver's seat! There was a revised interior with a split rear seat, this allowed seating for an adult and small child or an adult with luggage by raising the child seat. KR 200s now had interior trim panels and the driver's seat was fitted with map pockets. A new steering bar replaced the motorcycle type handlebar and the foot pedals were now the same as a normal car. Most importantly, the engine size was increased to 191cc, which produced 10.2bhp, although later cars had a reduction in power output.

The improved KR 200 received favourable reports from the Press, praising its handling and well-balanced chassis. Fend's rationale for the tandem seating arrangement, as opposed to the more conventional side-by- side layout, was to allow for a more

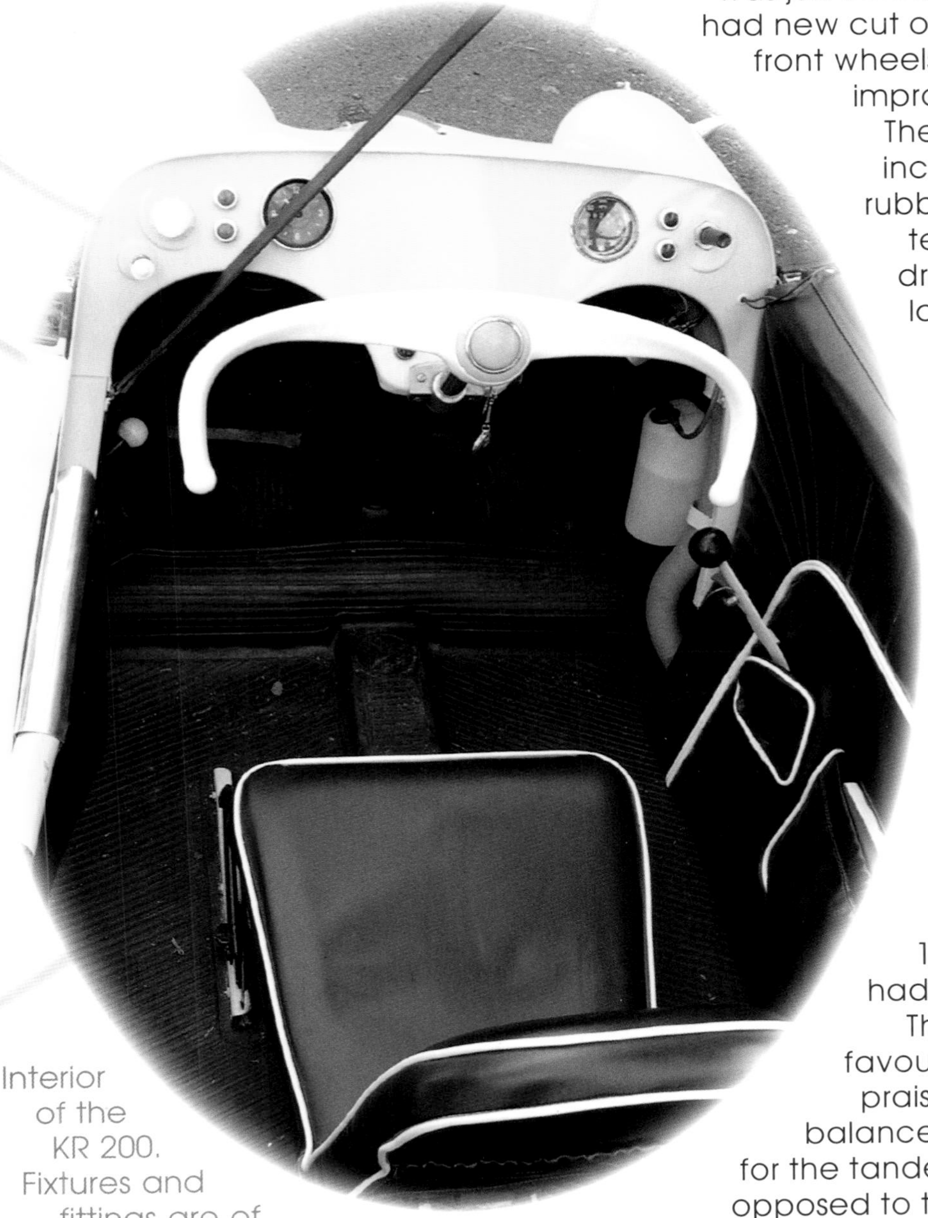

Interior of the KR 200. Fixtures and fittings are of good quality.

Engine cover tilted up to expose the two-stroke Fichtel and Sachs motor on this KR 200. The fuel tank, usually fixed to the lifting cover, has been removed in this picture.

streamlined low frontal area.

Fend decided to really prove the capabilities of the vehicle. On 29th August 1955, a KR 200 was driven around the Hockenheim race track circuit to demonstrate what it could do.

It was a twenty-four hour driving marathon undertaken by six different drivers. The car had a modified streamlined body with tiny cowled windscreen. The car maintained an average speed of 66.5mph, which was slightly less than the practice run of 71.5mph. Along the straight bits, the car did manage an impressive 77.7mph (125km/h). During the last few hours of the run, foggy conditions prevailed, which reduced the average speed to 59mph (95 km/h). Bales of straw were set alight and positioned to mark the edges of the track. The exercise was a success. The test proved that the car was reliable, sporty, safe and rugged enough for everyday use, and was great publicity. Indeed, 21 new endurance records were achieved. Targets set on the Montlhéry race track by a larger engined car of 350cc, were beaten by the Messerschmitt. It is also worth noting that most parts used were standard Messerschmitt, although the engine was tuned. 60kg of ballast was used to simulate the weight of a normal Messerschmitt with a passenger. One of the six drivers was Fritz Fend himself.

Nose badges. This is the original stylised eagle, which Mercedes Benz objected to.

Auto Union objected to the linking circles, claiming it was similar to its own emblem.

FMR finally settled on the three interlocking diamonds and nobody complained.

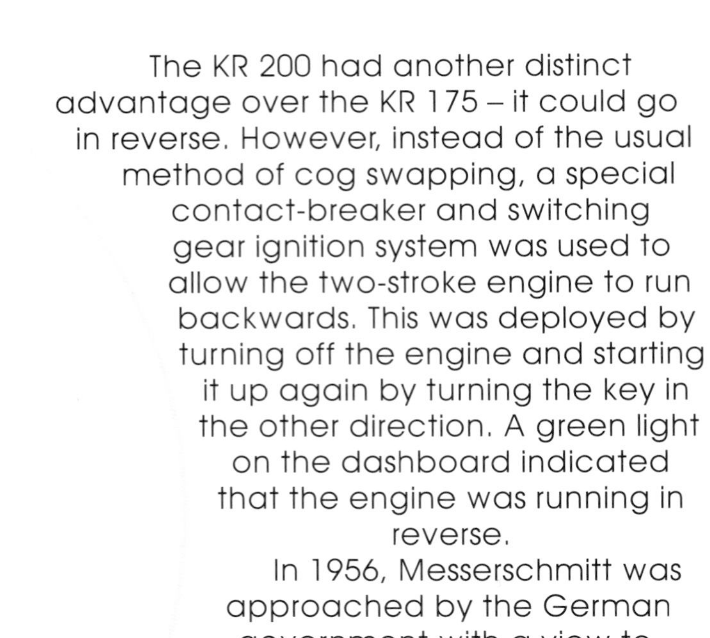

The KR 200 had another distinct advantage over the KR 175 – it could go in reverse. However, instead of the usual method of cog swapping, a special contact-breaker and switching gear ignition system was used to allow the two-stroke engine to run backwards. This was deployed by turning off the engine and starting it up again by turning the key in the other direction. A green light on the dashboard indicated that the engine was running in reverse.

In 1956, Messerschmitt was approached by the German government with a view to producing aircraft again. By now, Messerschmitt's car arm was making a loss and the government agreed to clear the debts if the car business were to be sold off.

The car arm was then bought by the state of Bavaria and divided up into smaller units. Messerschmitt allowed his name to still be used on the cars. Some 16,000 Messerschmitt KR 200s were made until December 1956. From late 1956/early 1957 until 1964, the cars were made by FMR, which stood for Fahrzeug und

160 'Tigers' are known to exist today.

The Tg 500 interior is surprisingly comfortable, thanks to the supportive front seat. Many KR 200 owners have fitted the Tg seat to their vehicles.

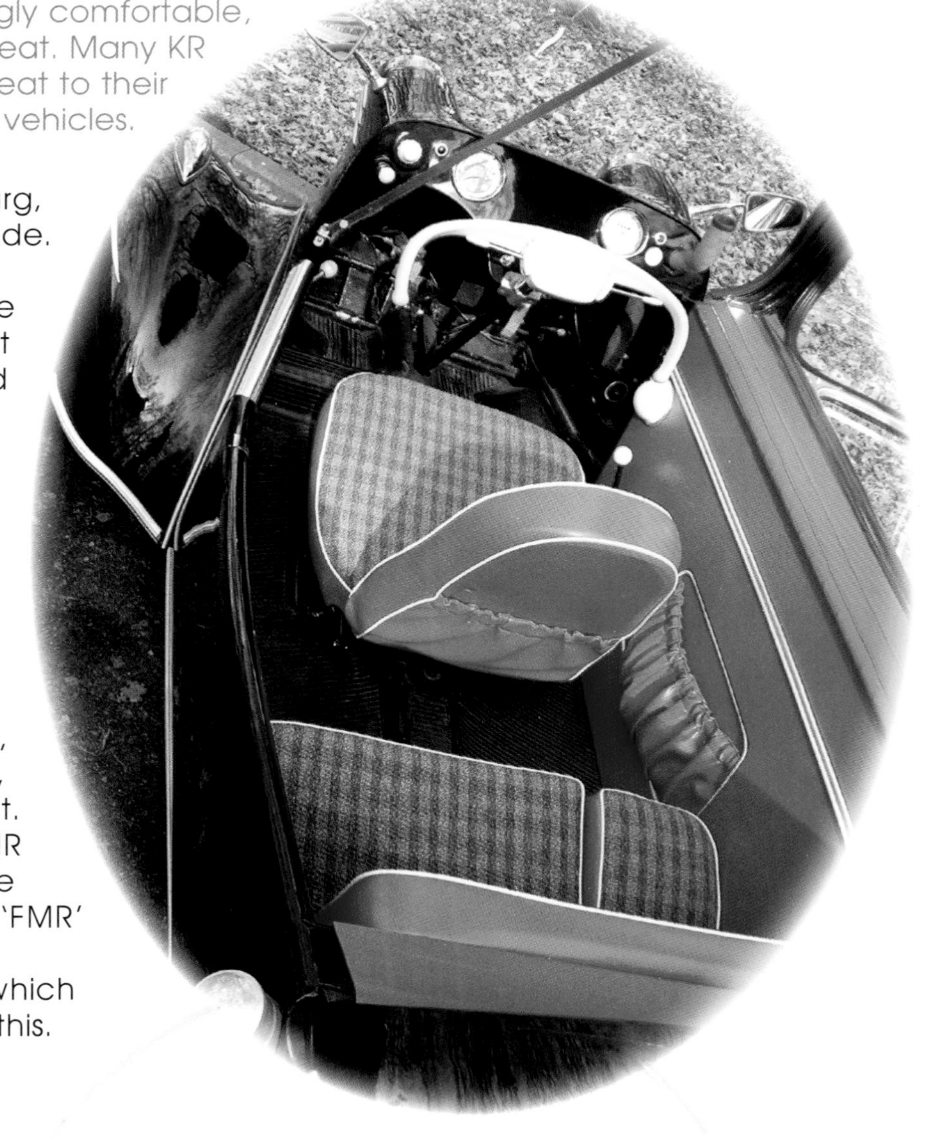

Maschinebau GMBH Regensburg, and around 25,000 cars were made. The chassis identity plate was designated as such, although the cars still carried the Messerschmitt badge on the side. Fend clubbed together with businessman Valentine Knott to buy the Regensburg company, done with the aid of the Bavarian State Bank. Fend was taken to court by Mercedes Benz over the logo on the nose section, which was the Regensburg Eagle, a sort of stylized bird. Mercedes claimed it was too similar to its own emblem, although it is difficult, in hindsight, to see what all the fuss was about. Mercedes won the case and FMR had to use another logo – three interlocking circles with the letters 'FMR' inside them.

Unfortunately, Auto-Union, which later became Audi, objected to this. The badge was then changed to interlocking diamonds, thus preventing further litigation.

There were variations in body styles. Most common was the domed top, but there was also a Roadster model, known as the KR 201, which came out in 1957.

The KR 201 had a folding hood instead of the dome and flexible sidescreens which could be removed easily.

The cabriolet of 1958 also had a fabric roof, but retained

the sliding windows and aluminium frame of the dome top models.

Many owners replaced their plexiglass domes with fabric roofs which were in some ways more practical. The domes were rather fragile and prone to cracking, and also tended to fry the heads of the car's occupants in warm weather.

Engine power output was reduced to 9.7bhp, which favoured German taxation classes. By the early 1960s, larger cars were more widely available and the demand for microcars was diminishing. Fend tried developing other kinds of vehicles, such as a twin-engined jeep, but this project never really got off the ground. To help boost sales, Fend had one more card up his sleeve. With the Hockenheim car still in his mind, Fend produced what can possibly be described as the ultimate Messerschmitt – the Tg 500.

Fend and Knott couldn't afford to develop a brand new vehicle, so they set about modifying the existing KR 200, giving it a broader appeal.

This new vehicle was called the Tg – Fend wanted to call it the Tiger, but for legal reasons, was unable to do so. However, the car did unofficially become

Cover removed to reveal the Tg 500 'Tiger' engine. This unit was manufactured by FMR, from parts supplied by other firms. This engine was also used in the Kultimax agricultural vehicle and the Australian Lightburn Zeta microcar.

Tg Sport model with tonneau cover and cut-down windscreen.

widely known as the Tiger.

The Tiger had four wheels and a 493cc twin-cylinder two-stroke Sachs engine mounted transversely in the tail. It produced 20bhp, and it was claimed the car could exceed 85mph. The 0-60 acceleration time was around fifteen seconds. Fuel consumption was around 45mpg, although probably a lot less when thrashed! There was also a 400cc version as well. The Tiger had independent rear suspension, using a single wishbone and coil spring for each wheel. The gearchange pattern was now a conventional 'H' gate, as opposed to the sequential movement of the KR 200 gearshift. No spinning the engine backwards to obtain reverse; on the Tiger, reverse gear was selected simply by moving the gear lever across towards the driver and forwards. Hydraulic brakes were used all around and the wheel size was 10in diameter, in comparison to the diminutive 8in wheels of the KR 200. Slightly larger wings were fitted to cope with the extra wheel size and wider track.

The Tiger was no true sports car with its tandem seating arrangement and unconventional steering bar. There was no synchromesh on the gearbox which made silent changes difficult to execute quickly. The car was not particularly noisy inside, but vibration coupled with the heavy direct steering made it tiring on long journeys. However, the Tiger was allegedly a fun car to drive, its ideal driver being one of cheerful disposition, enjoying its novelty value. One would imagine many impoverished KR 200 drivers setting their sights on a Tiger.

Sadly for the Tiger, and other microcars of the early 1960s, demand was dwindling. Fritz Fend left the company in November 1963 to become an independent consultant for Fichtel and Sachs and others. Cars such as the Mini and Volkswagen Beetle were relatively cheap, and people wanted conventional cars.

Production of the Tiger finished in 1964. The last three-wheeled KR 200 also left the Regensburg factory in this year. Altogether, over 50,000 Kabinenrollers were made, of all types. Nearly 11,000 of these were KR 175s. From 1955, an estimated 6800 KR 200s were imported into the UK. No one knows exactly how many Tigers were made, but it could possibly be in the region of 300-400 cars. 160 Tigers are known to exist today. It is interesting to note that the Tiger – officially known as the Tg – cannot be called a Messerschmitt, because it was built by FMR. The car was not authorized to bear the Messerschmitt name. Unlike the KR 200, the Tiger does not have the Messerschmitt scripted badge on the lifting section.

A KR 200 Dometop in excellent condition.

Goggomobil

The Goggomobil was the creation of Hans Glas and was made at Dingolfing, Bavaria. There were Spanish and Australian derivatives. In Australia, Goggomobils were imported by Buckle Motors of Sydney, New South Wales, minus their bodies. Fibreglass bodies, replicas of the steel originals, were then fitted by Buckle. Bill Buckle, the garage owner's son, enlisted the help of Stan Brown, a local engineer. Stan had designed one-off racing cars and between them they came up with the Dart, a sports car based on the Goggomobil floorpan. Approximately 700 of these Darts were sold.

Goggomobils were generally reliable and gave reasonable performance, considering the tiny engine size. Glas had been making scooters with Iso engines since 1951, but it wasn't until the mid-1950s that the company ventured into making cars.

Goggomobil T300.

In 1955, the Goggomobil T250 was made. The scooter manufacturing rights were then sold on to the Tula company of the USSR. The prototype Goggo had a front opening door like the Isetta, even though it had a bonnet of sorts. It did have four seats, but access to the rear was awkward, because the front door was the only means of entry. You then had to climb around the front seat to get to the back. When full-scale production took place, the cars simply used conventional side doors. The vehicle was compact, with an overall length of 9ft 6in (290 cm). The engine was Glas's own rear-mounted two-stroke twin-engine, of 247cc capacity. This little unit produced 14bhp with a top speed of around 50mph. In the UK, the slightly larger-engined car, the T300 was available. This engine produced 15bhp. Germany stuck to the T250, as the smaller engine allowed favourable tax concessions. Production of the T250 ceased in 1956, having made 25,000 cars. In 1957, the T300 gained two windscreen wipers, wind-up windows and was now known as the Regent in the UK. This year also saw the arrival of a coupé version in TS 300 or TS 400 guise. It was quite stylish considering its short length, and was

A later Goggomobil. Early Goggomobils had rear-hinged doors. The prototype had a single front opening door like the Isetta – rear passengers had to be quite nimble to clamber onto the back seat. This idea was abandoned on production models.

The very pretty Goggomobil Coupé was introduced in 1957.

dubbed the Mayfair. This little vehicle could touch 62mph. There was even a Getrag electro-magnetic pre-selector gearbox option on this car in the UK. By 1958, 100,000 Goggomobils had been made.

A van version was now available with a useful 250kg payload and sliding door. It was favoured by the German Post Office but quite rare in the UK. There was also a pickup. Hans Glas tried producing cars with 600cc and 700cc engines, some of which were two and four-cylinder water-cooled types. 87,575 of these were built. However, developing a new type of engine was expensive and these larger units were less reliable than the earlier two-strokes. Glas ran into financial difficulties and BMW took over production in 1967. The last Goggomobils had BMW on the chassis plate. Hans Glas died in

The Goggomobil two-stroke twin-cylinder engine was a willing performer, despite its size.

1968, aged 78. The smaller Goggomobils remained in production until 1969, for the German market. In total, 280,000 Goggomobils were made.

Goggomobil Coupé interior.

NOBEL

The Nobel was essentially a Fuldamobil built under licence in the UK. Fuldamobils were German-made fibreglass three-wheelers, powered by the Fichtel and Sachs unit as found in the Messerschmitt. The first Fuldamobils were manufactured by Norbert Stevenson, a caravan maker. These early cars were made of plywood, wood frames and steel panels. The N2 had hammered aluminium panels and had a Fichtel and Sachs 395cc engine. The earlier cars used a 248cc Baker and Polling unit, which was bolted directly to the floor and caused a lot of vibration for the occupants. Other Fuldamobils followed; a more rounded version with aluminium bodywork and later a fibreglass version in

A Nobel 200 pictured at a rally.

A three-wheeled Nobel made for the UK.

1957. This new version, which became the S7, was lighter and therefore gave greater performance. The car was available in Germany until 1969, although microcar sales were in decline by the early 1960s, and around 700 Fuldamobil S7s were sold. The Heinkel 198cc engine was fitted to Attica/Greek cars after 1965. Only 100 of these were made, but the car did live on with a restyled bodyshell, as the Alta in Greece until 1977. Licensed production of the Fuldamobil occurred in Holland. The car was known as the Bambino. There was also licensed production in Sweden (Fram King Fulda), Norway, Chile and Argentina (Bambi), India (Hans Vahaar) and Greece (Attica and later Alta). Fuldamobil production was probably more widespread worldwide than any other microcar.

The Nobel was introduced to the UK in 1958. York Nobel Industries, the former Heinkel concessionaires, were responsible for the project. Cyril Lord, the owner of the company, gave financial backing and Nobels became available ready-made or as a kit. Buying a kit car meant paying less purchase tax and labour costs; this must have been an asset to someone with limited funds looking to acquire a new car in the 1950s and 60s. The Fichtel and Sachs engine was used and the fibreglass car was mounted on a tubular steel frame with plywood floor. As with the Messerschmitt, the Nobel had the facility to run the engine backwards, as a means of reverse gear. Nobels were available with a single rear wheel or two wheels close together. Blue and white was the usual body colour. Nobels did have problems with cracking along the roofline, so this was modified, and the roof-mounted indicators were relocated to the front and rear. The cable brakes were not very efficient, which did little to help dwindling sales. Cyril Lord hoped to produce 400 cars a week. However, only around 1000 cars were made in total until 1962, when production ceased. Dealers had trouble getting rid of the cars. Nobels were still hanging around in showrooms two or three years after production ended.

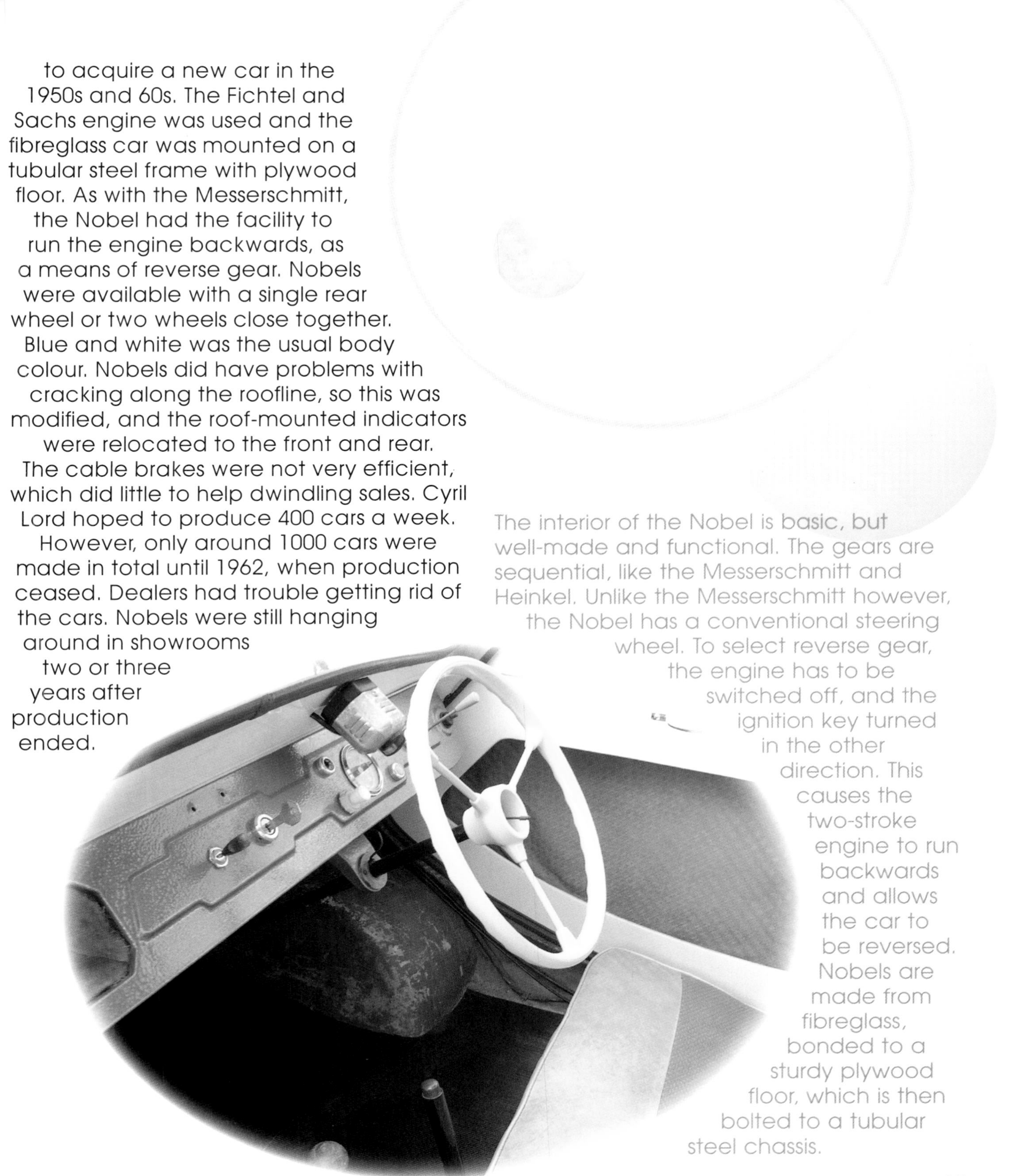

The interior of the Nobel is basic, but well-made and functional. The gears are sequential, like the Messerschmitt and Heinkel. Unlike the Messerschmitt however, the Nobel has a conventional steering wheel. To select reverse gear, the engine has to be switched off, and the ignition key turned in the other direction. This causes the two-stroke engine to run backwards and allows the car to be reversed. Nobels are made from fibreglass, bonded to a sturdy plywood floor, which is then bolted to a tubular steel chassis.

A four-wheeled Nobel. Chassis were supplied by Rubery Owen of Birmingham, England. The fibreglass reinforced polyester bodyshells were made by the Bristol Aeroplane Company, which also made boats. A method of pressure impregnation was used to layer up the fibreglass materials on these bodyshells. This was a procedure used on small components. Unfortunately, this method was less successful on the bodyshell of the Nobel, so the manufacturer reverted to layering up the fibreglass by hand. This was far more labour intensive, but produced a better quality result. The Bristol Aeroplane Company tried to charge Nobel more money to cover increasing costs, but Nobel, instead, turned to Short Brothers and Harland Ltd. Up until this point, Short had been assembling the cars in Belfast.

The interior of the Nobel is basic, but well made and functional. The gears are sequential, like the Messerschmitt and Heinkel. Unlike the Messerschmitt, the Nobel has a conventional steering wheel. However, to obtain reverse gear, the engine has to be switched off, and the ignition key turned in the other direction. This causes the two-stroke engine to run backwards and the car to be reversed. Nobels are made from fibreglass, which is bonded to a sturdy plywood floor, which is then bolted to a tubular steel chassis.

BERKELEY

The caravan maker, Berkeley, had been using fibreglass since 1948. It was no surprise then that Charles Panter, the managing director, should agree to build a tiny sports car after a meeting with the Minicar designer Lawrence Bond. In 1956, three prototypes were built. These were four-wheelers made of fibreglass and had 322cc Anzani two-stroke twin-cylinder engines fitted at the front. The cars were also front-wheel drive. Although the engines only produced 15bhp, the cars were nippy, due to their light weight. Anzani-engined cars were known as the Sports SA322 and proved to be popular. Unfortunately,

A four-wheeled Berkeley with a three-cylinder engine.

there were problems obtaining the engines, so Panter opted for the 328cc Excelsior two-stroke engine which produced 18bhp. This was known as the SE328 and later the B65, because it could do 65mph. The car also handled well and had excellent braking. In 1958, the B90 was introduced and, as the name suggests, could achieve 90mph. The B90 had a 492cc three-cylinder two-stroke Excelsior engine. A four-seater was introduced, called the Foursome.

In 1959, Panter introduced the B95 and the B105, aiming at the American market. A four-stroke Royal Enfield twin-cylinder 692cc engine was used, offering either 40bhp, or 50bhp, depending on

The 328cc Excelsior engine of the Berkeley T90 gave good performance.

A Berkeley T60 seen here with its owner.

the customer's preference. The front end had to be restyled slightly, with a squarer grille, to accommodate the larger engine. In October of this same year, the T60 was launched.

The T60 was similar to the B65, with a modified rear end and single rear wheel. The T60 sold really well; 1850 cars were sold in the first year of production, compared to the B65 selling only 2310 in total. This was probably due to the fact that three-wheelers enjoyed tax concessions in Britain.

Unfortunately, Berkeley's caravan sales were not doing well and the car arm was thus affected. Berkeley had legal wrangles with the firm Bakelite, which it claimed was responsible for poor quality materials,

Seen part-way through a restoration, the Berkeley B90 displays its 492cc Excelsior triple. The firm switched to Excelsior after having supply problems with British Anzani. This B90 produces 30bhp. The fuel tank (not present on this car) was usually mounted under the bonnet with a gravity feed system to the carburettors.

resulting in the blistering of the glassfibre bodywork. Berkeley's finances were in a sorry state by this time and Bakelite made a successful counter-claim against it. Despite launching a new car, called the Bandit, the firm called it a day in 1960. A total of 2500 four-wheeled Berkeleys and 1800 three-wheelers were made by the Biggleswade firm. Berkeleys today have an enthusiastic following, with some owners modifying their cars to accommodate mini or Citroën 2CV engines. The old factory site has recently been developed into a residential area and only the name remains.

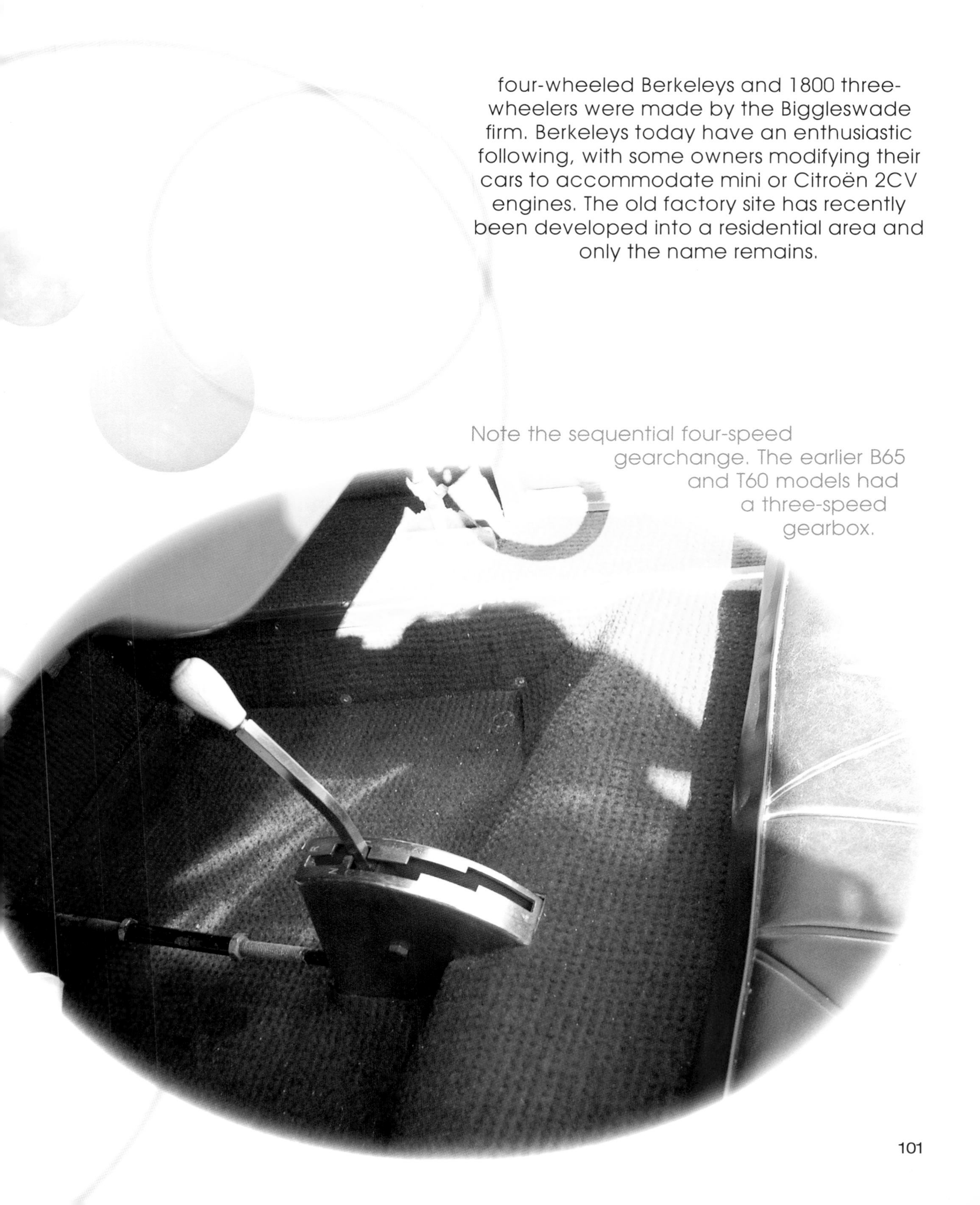

Note the sequential four-speed gearchange. The earlier B65 and T60 models had a three-speed gearbox.

More of a sports car than a microcar, the Berkeley looks stylish from any angle.

MICROCARS TODAY

As fuel becomes more expensive and roads become more crowded, the need for small vehicles will only increase. Until a fully integrated, efficient public transport system is in place, small cars will be the first choice for many. Modern microcars are everywhere, all around the world. The Piaggio Ape (pronounced 'appy') van, the similar Vespa van and pickup trucks are used widely in Italy and parts of France. In countries like India and Bangladesh, the 'Tuk-Tuk' or Bajaj motor rickshaws are omnipresent and

The chic and successful Smart.

The Piaggio Ape truck – rare in the UK, but popular in France and Italy as a utility vehicle.

An Aixam microcar.

plying for trade. Elsewhere in Europe, and slowly creeping into the United States, the Smart car shows off its chic appeal on the city streets. French micros such as Aixam and Ligier can be seen in the UK, their 500cc diesel engines working hard to keep up with the flow of traffic. Although not such a common sight on the roads nowadays, the Citroën 2CV can still be seen bouncing along the lanes as practical transport. The new breed of microcar has become more of a trendy accessory – a stylish town runabout rather than bread and butter motoring for hard up motorcyclists who don't want to get wet. The Smart has a very technically advanced specification. Electronic fuel management and a three-cylinder alloy engine developed by Mercedes, is the order of the day. The bodyshell consists of detachable polypropelene panels on a space frame. This space frame is designed to absorb an impact, giving the car an enviable safety record.

A tiny hi-tech sports car of only 656cc engine capacity, the Beat from Honda was imported into the UK in the early 1990s. The Beat was a fun vehicle, being a mid-engined convertible. Suzuki brought out the Cappuccino around the same time, with its 657cc engine. Similar in concept to the Honda, the tiny Suzuki resembled a smaller version of the Mazda MX5. Cappuccinos are still being imported today. These cars meet the specification limits for Japan's Kei-jidosha or 'K' class, which means they are no longer than 3 metres and have an engine capacity of no more than 660cc. With space at a premium in urban areas around the world, the demand for small cars has never been greater. It looks like the modern microcar is here to stay.

INDEX

Agg 45
Agg, Peter 44, 49
Aixam 105
Allard Clipper 7
Alta 94
Americo Emilio Romi 10
Ape Truck – see under Piaggio
and Vespa van 74, 103, 104
Ashley, Captain Ron J 11
Attica 94
Austin A35 13
Austin Seven 7, 71
Auto Union 83, 85
Avonex Group 74

Bajaj Autorickshaw 103
Bakelite 99, 100
Baker and Polling 93
Balkan Roads to Istanbul 52
Bambi 94
Bean 74
Benz 7
Berkeley
- Berkeley 97-103
- Berkeley Bandit 100
- Berkeley B65 98, 99, 101
- Berkeley B90 98, 100
- Berkeley Foursome 98
- Berkeley SE 328 98
- Berkeley T60 99,101

BMC 2
BMW
- BMW 7-11
- BMW Isetta 9-32
- BMW 600 12, 15, 19, 20
- BMW 700 13, 19

Bond
- Bond 61-71
- Bond Bug 8, 68, 70, 73
- Bond Equipe 74
- Bond, Lawrence 61, 97
- Bond Minicar 61-68
- Bond Ranger Van 68, 69
- Bond 875 68, 69
- MKA 61-64
- MKB 64
- MKC 65
- MKD 65
- MKE 66
- MKF 67
- MKG 66, 67

Bradshaw Companies 61
Brands Hatch 68
Brighton Isetta Factory 31

Bristol Aeroplane Company 96
British Anzani
(also Anzani) 50, 56, 97, 100
Brown, Henry 50, 55
Brown, Stan 89
Bubble car 7, 8, 32, 33
Buckle, Bill 89

Cannell, Cyril 60
Champion microcar 32
Citroën 2CV 8, 11, 44, 101, 105
Craven and Hendrick
of New York 66

Dingolfing 89
DKW 58-60
Donath, Kurt 32
Dundalk Engineering 39, 41, 44

Elva Courier 47
Excelsior 98, 100

Fend Flitzer 79
Fend, Fritz 75, 82, 88
Fiat 500 10, 44
Fichtel and Sachs 79, 82, 88, 93
FMR 83-86
Fuldamobil 44, 93, 94,
Fuldamobil N2 93

Girling 11, 67
Glas, Hans 89, 91, 92
Glen Investments 74
Goggomobil
Goggomobil 89-92
Goggomobil/Buckle Dart 89
Goggomobil Coupé 90-93
Goggomobil Mayfair 91
Goggomobil Regent 90
Goggomobil T250 90
Goggomobil T300 89, 90
Grant, Cary 26
Gray, CR Lieutenant Colonel 64

Heinkel
Heinkel, Ernst 32, 34, 38, 39
Heinkel Kabine 32-49
Heinkel Pearle moped 48
Heinkel Touriste Scooter 33, 34
Hillman Imp 68, 69
Hockenheim 82, 86
Hoffmann Auto-kabine 11
Hoffmann, Jakob 11
Honda Beat 106
Hunslet 50, 55

Isetta (see also under BMW Isetta) 9-31

K Class 106
Karen, Tom 70
Knott, Valentine 85, 86
Kultimax 86

Lambretta 44, 45, 49
Lightburn Zeta 86
Ligier 74, 105
Lincoln and Nolan 41
Lord, Cyril 94, 95
Lord, Leonard 8

Manxcar 56
Mazda MX5 106
Mercedes Benz 83, 85
Messerschmitt
Messerschmitt 75-88
Messerschmitt, Willi 79
Messerschmitt KR 175 75, 78-81, 84
Messerschmitt KR 200 75, 78, 81, 82-88
Messerschmitt KR 201 85
Messerschmitt Tg 500 84-88
Minicar 7
MIRA 53
Motte, Nel and Peter 52

Nichols, Frank 47
Nobel 93-96
Noble Motors 40, 47

Ogle Design 73

Panter, Charles 97, 98
Peel
Peel 56-60
Peel Trident 59, 60
P50 56-60
Presley, Elvis 26

Raleigh Safety Seven 71
Regensburg 79, 85, 88
Reliant
Reliant 8, 70-74
Reliant Anadol 74
Reliant Rebel 70-72
Reliant Regal 70-73
Reliant Robin 71, 73, 74
Reliant Scimitar 74
Reliant TW9 73
Rodley 50
Royal Enfield 98

Saab two-stroke 33
Scootacar 50-55
Selectroshift 27
Sharp's Bearcub 66
Smart 8, 103, 105, 106
Speyer 38, 40
Stevenson, Norbert 93
Suez Crisis 7, 38
Surtees, John 68
Suzuki Capuccino 106

Tamworth 70, 71, 74
Tempo 32
Tro-bike 45
Tro-kart 45
Tro-tent 45
Tro-tractor 45
Trojan (see also under Heinkel) 32-49
Trojan Utility 49

Velam 10, 11, 27, 29
Vespa 10, 60, 103
Vespa van 103
Vidal and Sohn 32, 38
Villiers engine 50, 51, 53, 55, 61, 65, 67, 68
Volkswagen Beetle 88

Williams, TL 71

York Nobel 41, 44, 94

Zuffenhausen factory 38